LOTUS
BEAUTY

by Satinder Kaur Chohan

‖SAMUEL FRENCH‖

FOR AMATEUR PRODUCTION ENQUIRIES

UNITED KINGDOM AND WORLD
EXCLUDING NORTH AMERICA
licensing@concordtheatricals.co.uk

020-7054-7298

Each title is subject to availability from Concord Theatricals, depending upon country of performance.

This work is published by Samuel French, an imprint of Concord Theatricals Ltd.

The Professional Rights in this play are controlled by Professional Performing Rights: applications for performance by professionals in any medium and in any language throughout the world should be addressed to Berlin Associates, www.berlinassociates.com email: agents@ berlinassociates.com

USE OF COPYRIGHTED MUSIC

A licence issued by Concord Theatricals to perform this play does not include permission to use the incidental music specified in this publication. In the United Kingdom: Where the place of performance is already licensed by the PERFORMING RIGHT SOCIETY (PRS) a return of the music used must be made to them. If the place of performance is not so licensed then application should be made to PRS for Music (www.prsformusic.com). A separate and additional licence from PHONOGRAPHIC PERFORMANCE LTD (www.ppluk.com) may be needed whenever commercial recordings are used. Outside the United Kingdom: Please contact the appropriate music licensing authority in your territory for the rights to any incidental music.

USE OF COPYRIGHTED THIRD-PARTY MATERIALS

Licensees are solely responsible for obtaining formal written permission from copyright owners to use copyrighted third-party materials (e.g., artworks, logos) in the performance of this play and are strongly cautioned to do so. If no such permission is obtained by the licensee, then the licensee must use only original materials that the licensee owns and controls. Licensees are solely responsible and liable for clearances of all third-party copyrighted materials, and shall indemnify the copyright owners of the play(s) and their licensing agent, Concord Theatricals Ltd., against any costs, expenses, losses and liabilities arising from the use of such copyrighted third-party materials by licensees.

IMPORTANT BILLING AND CREDIT REQUIREMENTS

If you have obtained performance rights to this title, please refer to your licensing agreement for important billing and credit requirements.

LOTUS BEAUTY was first produced by Hampstead Downstairs/Celia Atkin, in association with Tamasha Theatre Company on 13th May 2022. The performance was directed by Pooja Ghai, Assistant Director Cassia Thakkar, Designer Rosa Maggiora, lighting by Matt Haskins, Sound by The Ringham Brothers, Costume Supervisor Malena Arcucci, Dialect Gurkiran Kaur. The cast was as follows:

PINKY . . . . Anshula Bain

BIG DHADHI . . . . Souad Faress

TANWANT . . . . Zainab Hasan

KAMAL . . . . Ulrika Krishnamurti

REITA . . . . Kiran Landa

AUTHOR'S NOTES

Whether in Jackson Heights, New York, Delhi, India or Southall, West London, the Asian woman's beauty salon symbolises the global makeover of Asian women, cross-pollinating Eastern and Western shades of beauty.

Set in my hometown of Southall, West London, *Lotus Beauty* is inspired by the multi-generational women of British Asian suburbia and the vibrant ladies-only salons they frequent. In these salons, women go to pamper and preen themselves, sharing their struggles, gossiping and waxing lyrical about their successes, in safe spaces that offer sanctuary and community with other women. But scratch below the polished suburban veneer and a deeper malaise runs beneath. *Lotus Beauty* seeks to peel away the hidden layers of what it means to be Asian and female in modern Britain, holding up a mirror to see the light and shadows reflecting back.

As a Sikh, I had been raised never to cut my hair or remove my body hair. 'Kesh' (hair), one of the five K's in Sikhism, is regarded as a sacred source of divine creation and spiritual strength. For Sikh girls like me, blessed with abundant jet-black hair, playground taunts like 'Brezhnev eyebrows', 'hairy mush', 'Elvis sideburns' abounded. As a teen, I secretly began removing my facial hair and shaving my legs (playing junior tennis made hairy brown legs a big no!)/As a late teen, I discovered the joys of threading at my regular salon – *The Beauty Room*, which had grown from a tiny space in Southall's Liberty Market into a thriving space of its own in nearby Heston. (I eventually did an inspiring month's research/working stint there, interviewing female clients about their lives and experiences, which fed into early drafts of the play).

In Southall, I had also grown up with urban myths about the women in white who haunted the local train tracks and roads around Southall Station, sadly rooted in real-life tragic stories. In 2005, one such devastating suicide made national headlines. Navjeet Sidhu, 27, jumped to her death at Southall Station, holding her 5-year-old daughter and 23-month-old son. Six months later, Navjeet's grieving mother killed herself in the same spot.

In 2007, when I first conceived the play in the long, stuttering journey from page to stage – 80 out of 240 rail suicides in Britain, occurred on the stretch of track running through Southall, Slough and other Asian areas. Living in one of those neighbourhoods, one sadly becomes desensitised to the desperate ends chosen by those women, many victims of emotional, physical and sexual violence and abuse but also more recently, male immigrants crushed by broken UK dreams. While 'person under a train' or 'person on the track' is a mere inconvenience for disrupted commuters, the tragic loss of life is brushed over and forgotten too quickly. *Lotus Beauty* remembers them.

With all its beauty and spiritual connotations – the blooming lotus flower growing out of muddy waters – the lotus seemed a perfect metaphor for the play. The play also draws on Homer's *The Odyssey* and Alfred Tennyson's poem *The Lotos Eater*s, exploring how some (British) Asians have become modern 'Lotus Eaters', settling into a 'lotophagi' (state of blissful forgetfulness) of who they are and where they come from. In the muddy capitalist swamps of modern Britain, they gorge themselves on a lotus of image, money, materialism, obsessing about how they look, how much they earn, what they own –a 21st century narcosis, spiritual bankruptcy and rampant individualism, which admittedly affects us all.

In *Lotus Beauty*, this cosmetic living manifests through characters disconnected from deeper selves and each other. These are women who become each other's worst enemies, complicit in one another's suffering, absolving husbands/brothers/sons/father-in-laws of harmful actions, while masking the true weight and wounds of the emotional labour and immigrant/colonial trauma they must carry disproportionately over generations.

The play suggests that beauty is about letting superficial masks drop – by truly facing ourselves, facing others, sharing pain and healing those deeper wounds. In this way, perhaps it is possible to begin breaking ingrained cycles of inherited and lived immigrant/colonial trauma, so we not only heal as individuals but as families and communities too. Maybe then, women like Navjeet Sidhu can fully bloom, like the spirited, resilient women the play celebrates. These are the women who have overcome struggles as women and immigrants in Britain, lifting themselves up and others too.

But even for these pioneering women, even if the deepest wounds may carry the greatest pain, their healing may carry the greatest beauty too, which will always run more than skin (colour) deep. Without mud, there is no lotus.

NOTE FOR CREATIVES

The stage directions, use of clients, props, sound (and regularity) of trains and music indicate the everyday workings of the Salon. These can be more freely interpreted by creatives (to build the story and atmosphere) when staging the play.

more back a page →

CHARACTERS

REITA – Salon owner, in her 40s

TANWANT – Salon worker, in her mid-30s

PINKY – Reita's daughter, 15

BIG DHADHI – Reita's mother-in-law, in her 70s

KAMAL – Salon client, in her late 20s

(**CLIENTS** can be played by doubling cast members.)

•

ACT ONE

Opening

(A winter's morning. Lotus Beauty Salon is rooted in Southall in deepest British Asian suburbia, close to the local train tracks. Rain crashes against the glass exterior. Magic lantern images of Asian beauty queens dance around a mirrored, pink panelled interior. An Asian radio station warbles a 1960s romantic Hindi film song, telling of longing, love and loss*. At the back, floor-to-ceiling blinds hang either side of a glass door, glimpsing a grey street outside. In the centre of the door, a stained-glass pink lotus glows brightly, below a hanging 'Open/Closed' sign set to 'Closed'.)

(On the right, there is a small reception area, with a desk and swivel chair. The desk is topped with a telephone, open-paged diary and plastic holder, stashed with Lotus Beauty *salon leaflets. On the left, neatly arranged chairs sit next to a magazine rack spilling over with Asian and Western women's magazines. Downstage left, there are two*

---

* A licence to produce LOTUS BEAUTY does not include a performance licence for any third-party or copyrighted music. Licensees should create an original composition or use music in the public domain. For further information, please see Music Use Note on page iii.

adjoining cubicles. One cubicle is slid shut. The other is open – during work moments and transitions, clients can be glimpsed as silhouettes in the cubicles.)

(In the foreground, chairs sit either side of a manicure table. On the far right, beauty products line a small-shelved wall, bookended by kitsch Indian Goddess statues. A large walled mirror hangs above. Downstage right, a draped opening leads to an unseen backroom/kitchen area. The salon interior looks bright and modern.)

(A distant high-speed train cuts through the magic lantern images and song, revealing **REITA**, *in a neat pink uniform. She polishes the mirror obsessively with a cloth, before getting distracted by her reflection.* **REITA** *speaks in an affected British accent, betraying Indian undertones.* **TANWANT** *speaks in a heavy Indian accent.)*

REITA. *(Analysing her face.)* Bags?

*(***TANWANT** *emerges from the cubicle in a slightly dishevelled pink uniform.)*

TANWANT. Weight of being woman, hunnah?

REITA. Big bags.

TANWANT. Use desi potion I tell you bout. Big bag, dark circle, vanish no time –

REITA. *(Panicking.)* 'Dark circles'?

TANWANT. *(Spotting a grey hair on* **REITA**.*)* Reita, nother grey hair?

REITA. *(Panicking.)* Where?

TANWANT. *(Pretending not to notice.)* Nahi, nahi, is the light!

REITA. *(Spotting the grey hair.)* More?

TANWANT. What you s'pect at sixty? Turn blonde?

REITA. Tanni, I'm in my menopausal forties. Not my pensioned off sixties.

TANWANT. Same thing no?

REITA. Sixty one dreaded day...

TANWANT. No lifetime guarantee.

> *(**REITA** yanks out a grey hair.)*

Dye, hide but never, ever pull grey hair! Mummyji always said, "Pull one, whole garden grow."

> *(**REITA** hands **TANWANT** a pot of bleach.)*

REITA. Quick, before opening. *(Drops in a chair.)* Bleach double, triple, if you have to!

TANWANT. I got client first thing –

REITA. I'm the boss.

TANWANT. *(Preparing the bleach.)* OK, I bleaching –

REITA. Lighten every dark line, bag, wrinkle, age spot, liver spot –

TANWANT. I lightening –

REITA. *(Points around her face.)* Here, there –

TANWANT. *(Stops.)* I know what to do.

> *(**TANWANT** resumes preparing the bleach. Pause.)*

REITA. How did I get as old as her?

TANWANT. Who?

REITA. My mother.

>   *(Once she finishes mixing,* **TANWANT** *applies the bleach.)*

TANWANT. When we little, we look up to our Mummyji. Never think we reach her age. When she thirty, for us, like she sixty. Forty, like she seventy. Fifty, like a one hundred. Then we her age and say, "You not know? Thirty is new twenty. Forty is new thirty." So if you forty five, really you thirty five and I thirty five, so really I twenty five...or fifteen? ...What your Mummyji was like?

>   *(A distant high-speed train zips past, rattling the cubicle. A small piece of ceiling drops on* **REITA***'s partially bleached face.)*

REITA. Ow!

>   *(***REITA** *and* **TANWANT** *look up.)*

TANWANT. Hai, ceiling's peeling... wait, it's stuck in the bleach!

>   *(***TANWANT** *removes a ceiling piece from* **REITA***'s bleach.)*

REITA. *(Getting up.)* I only plastered it last month.

>   *(***REITA** *pushes against the wall.)*

Bloody trains. Sound-proofing has stopped working.

TANWANT. Get Harmeet Bhaji to take a look. Cos he not working either.

REITA. He's busy looking for work every day.

TANWANT. *(Bites her tongue.)* A-ho.

REITA. My salon – I'll take care of it. *(Sitting back down.)* But I'll be out of this dead-end town long before that.

TANWANT. Still look hain?

REITA. Won't stop 'til I find my dream house. In fact, I met Councillor Gill last night –

TANWANT. Fancy lady who never work for Southall peoples who vote her?

REITA. She might be selling one of her houses *and* a perfect space for a new salon.

TANWANT. In dead-end town?

REITA. Upmarket town nearby – with a wealthier clientele.

TANWANT. We poor no good no more?

REITA. I've worked hard to move up – and out.

> (**REITA** *taps her face.* **TANWANT** *resumes bleaching.*)

TANWANT. Quickie bleach me after I quickie bleach you?

REITA. Barely got time for this.

TANWANT. *(Stops bleaching.)* I black iron thava. Burnt roti. How future husband who save me s'pose to see me?

REITA. Do it yourself, after work.

TANWANT. Your bleaching like healing massage –

REITA. No time.

TANWANT. You say we walking ad in salon. Look this face. What ad this is?

REITA. Bleach.

TANWANT. *(Bleaching.)* Punjabis want wheat colour girl... to chew up... spit out... Chotte buffaloes! Nahi, forget wheat, I want fair 'n' lovely gori gori rang like you –

REITA. Born in the wrong country.

TANWANT. You born there too.

REITA. Born there, belong here. *(Points to face to prove it.)* Gori gori rang.

> *(***TANWANT*** *stops bleaching* ***REITA***, *letting the bleach rest.* ***REITA*** *and* ***TANWANT*** *prepare the salon for opening.)*

TANWANT. Today, I might meet him very first time.

REITA. In a ladies-only salon?

TANWANT. Could happen when I get lunch from Kulcha Cottage.

REITA. You bring a home-cooked Tupperware every day.

TANWANT. When I finish work then – if I not too dark for him to see me.

REITA. Be married two decades, you'll be invisible to each other anyway.

TANWANT. Nahi, I bet Harmeet tell you how much he love you everyday.

REITA. I've no time for gupshup.

TANWANT. S'not gupshup. Romantic – how husband should behave.

> *(***REITA*** *looks closely at* ***TANWANT****'s face.)*

REITA. It is dark isn't it? You should burn the roots right out – with a laser.

TANWANT. When? Too busy with work, finding husband...

REITA. Get Pinky to do it –

TANWANT. Burn my face right off?

REITA. *(Looking at her phone clock.)* She's late again.

TANWANT. Reita, how long I look him?

REITA. 'Til you realise you don't need him.

TANWANT. If I earn more, I buy British husband with passport tomorrow –

REITA. "If you earn more" ...?

TANWANT. I work here three-year already, no one panny pay rise –

REITA. Cash in hand, tax-free –?

TANWANT. When you get new salon, I get pay rise?

REITA. If I take you with me –

TANWANT. I no go?

>   *(Silence.)*

On bus here, I see men on Dyer Street, Ehni thand, stand there, thin jacket, rain soak skin, work hand grip rip pocket, wait all day for builder job. Proud farmer come all this way to freeze? Starve? Beg?

REITA. No work, yet they peck at the pavement like pigeons.

TANWANT. When I take bus back, still they wait. Then, late night, apnay girls take their place, wait for dirty mans pay them do dirty job.

REITA. Where do they all keep coming from?

TANWANT. Same place we all come from.

>   *(Blue police lights and blaring sirens ricochet around the salon.)*

Hai, what happen out there?

REITA. Don't move.

>   *(With her bleached face, **REITA** rushes out and disappears from view. **TANWANT** freezes on the spot, eyes closed, hands over her ears.)*

TANWANT. What if... what if...?

> *(Blue lights continue flashing. Sirens continue blaring.)*

(Shouts.) What happen out there?

> *(Silence.)*

(Shouts.) Reita?

> *(Silence.)*

Reita?

> *(**TANWANT** quickly slathers bleach over her face, slumps in the chair and covers herself with a towel. **REITA** rushes back in, locking the salon door.)*

REITA. They drove right past, down – *(Glares at **TANWANT**.)*

TANWANT. BD always say if police come, swap place with client ek dhum. Make client beautician, beautician client, then they check her, not you. *(Patting her face.)* Think I leave it on now.

REITA. *(Sighing)* We nearly done?

TANWANT. Thori left.

> *(**REITA** swaps places with **TANWANT**, who takes off **REITA**'s bleach.)*

REITA. You hear they raided *Reflections* the other day?

TANWANT. What? ...

REITA. Babita said immigration police *and* soldiers burst in like a SWAT team.

TANWANT. Swat what?

REITA. Soldiers were wearing army jackets, waving machine guns –

TANWANT. Gu-gu-guns?

REITA. Clients were on beds, half-naked, dripping in oil and wax. Soldiers marched five salon workers out in handcuffs. Whole street was watching.

TANWANT. Long as I with you, I no worry.

REITA. It's a huge fine, even a jail sentence – for me. But Pinky always says, "Tanwant is the fastest Freshie threader in the West."

TANWANT. *(Relieved.)* Blesses her.

REITA. Soon, I might not have a choice.

(**TANWANT** *finishes taking off* **REITA**'s *bleach.*)

TANWANT. *(Abruptly.)* There. You done.

REITA. *(Checking her phone clock.)* Opening time! I'll get the other cubicle ready. Tidy the magazines, refill the wax *(Hands* **TANWANT** *wax roller cartridge bottles.)* – warm wax, not cold wax, like yesterday. This isn't a church – it's a business – and button up.

(**REITA** *turns the shop sign from 'Closed' to 'Open', en route to the other cubicle. Holding the bottles,* **TANWANT** *composes herself. Tidying the magazines, she drops one and scans an article.)*

TANWANT. *(Points to the magazine.)* Oh look Reita. In China, police excute prisoner. Then beauty company buy prisoner body... and skin them. Use skin to make collagen lip and wrinkle cream. Try those product. Stop going round in dark circle. It show.

REITA. *(Peering from the cubicle.)* You'll grow old one day too.

TANWANT. *(Reading.)* Uh nahi. Cos here, say woman can inject dead foetus cell to stay young.

REITA. That's disgusting. *(Pause.)* Is it expensive?

TANWANT. Only rich can afford to stay young, stay beautiful, hunnah? Poor peoples grow old, grow ugly, too quick.

REITA. Where do they get the dead foetuses?

TANWANT. Better not know. Then you has clear skin with clear conscience – look twenty year younger.

REITA. *(Retreating into the cubicle.)* Could be a high-class treatment in the new salon…

TANWANT. Rabba, wish I keep my dead foetus now…

> *(The door rattles. A ghostly female figure drifts by.)*

REITA. *(Calling out.)* It's open!

> *(The door rattles again.)*

You check. Must be those dirty crackheads again.

> *(**KAMAL**'s face is pushed up against the lotus on the door, frozen in terror by **TANWANT**'s ghostly face. As **TANWANT** unlocks the door, **KAMAL** drops over the doorstep, breathless and soaked. **KAMAL** wears a dull-coloured shalwar kameez underneath a wet jacket, with white trainers. She speaks in an Indian accent.)*

TANWANT. Nahi, it's only Kamali.

KAMAL. *(Distressed.)* Sat Sri Akal.

TANWANT. Reita, your cleaner here!

REITA. *(Shouting from the cubicle.)* Kamal, take a seat.

> *(Dazed and agitated, **KAMAL** shuffles around. Eyeing up **KAMAL**, **TANWANT** sits at the desk, refilling wax bottles. **KAMAL** shakes off the rain, drying herself with a tissue. She takes*

a magazine from the rack, drops it, picks it up, stuffs it back, hoping **TANWANT** *has not noticed.* **TANWANT** *gets up to put the magazine neatly back.)*

TANWANT. Oi Kamali?

*(***KAMAL*** rubs her temples. She does not hear* **TANWANT.***)*

(Louder.) Oi Kamali? What happen out there?

*(***KAMAL*** shakes her head, staring blankly.)*

Blue light? You just come from outside.

KAMAL. Something... happened –

TANWANT. Where?

KAMAL. – at the – the station.

TANWANT. Station?

KAMAL. I – I got – late dropping Gaggan... to school... There were – police... ambulance... –

TANWANT. Sachi? What you see?

*(***KAMAL*** shakes her head.* **REITA** *emerges, from the cubicle.)*

KAMAL. *(Getting up, shaking, to* **REITA.***)* I came to collect my wage –

(Irked, **TANWANT** *heads into the cubicle to wipe off her bleach.)*

REITA. You ok?

KAMAL. *(Rubbing her temples.)* Hanji.

*(***REITA** *gives* **KAMAL** *money from her handbag.)*

REITA. *(Smiling.)* Your first wage –

KAMAL. *(Stuffing the money into her pocket.)* Thank you. *(Moves towards the door.)*

REITA. Kamal, sure you're ok?

> (**KAMAL** *stops and nods.*)

I'm waiting for my client, could give you a quick massage if you like…

KAMAL. *(Shaking her head.)* It's fine, thank you.

REITA. A bonus, perk of the job –

KAMAL. I can't take off my clothes.

REITA. No need for a head massage.

KAMAL. Too messy.

REITA. It's relaxing.

> (**KAMAL** *shakes her head.* **REITA** *is distracted by a pinging phone message.* **TANWANT** *returns bleach free.)*

(Reading her message.) Try something else. Tanni? *(Types on her phone.)*

TANWANT. *(Handing* **KAMAL** *a leaflet.)* At *Lotus Beauty*, we make plain woman look very beautiful. Make brand new you. We do it all – bleach, thread, wax, pedicure, laser, electrolysis, Epil Pro, IPL –

> (**KAMAL** *rubs her head.*)

Aroma facial, power facial, peel facial, oxygen facial, fruit facial, herbal facial, anti-age facial, foetal facial, deep cleanse treatment – to get rid of street dirt. Or pamper treatment? Reach parts husband never do.

KAMAL. *(Confused, backing towards the door.)* I should –

TANWANT. Simple womans do wax or thread first. Get rid of ugly facial hair.

KAMAL. *(Rubbing her head.)* I'm not good with pain.

TANWANT. Beauty hurts. You get used to it.

> *(**REITA** puts her phone away and leads **KAMAL** to the manicure table.)*

REITA. I'll do a quick manicure.

KAMAL. Oh *(Pause.)* ... Gaggan loves me painting her nails.

> *(**REITA** seats a tentative **KAMAL** at the table.)*

REITA. *(Picking up a bottle.)* Pink?

KAMAL. Her favourite colour...

> *(**REITA** files **KAMAL**'s nails, as **TANWANT** glares.)*

REITA. Kamal, you clean so well. My reflection stares right back. Clean our house too? I'll pay extra...

TANWANT. Harmeet got free time – why he never clean?

REITA. *(To **TANWANT**.)* Fix the dermabrasion machine in there.

TANWANT. You break 'gain?

REITA. Now.

> *(Cursing under her breath, **TANWANT** heads into the cubicle.)*

KAMAL. Yes. I'll clean your house too.

REITA. Great. We'll work out a good time for us both.

> *(**REITA** tends to **KAMAL**'s nails. Pause.)*

KAMAL. How strange, sitting here with you again.

REITA. "Again?"

KAMAL. You did my make-up and mehndi on my wedding day.

REITA. I did?

KAMAL. You don't remember?

REITA. Hot flushes, fading looks, fading memory...

KAMAL. I'd arrived from India – about six years ago –

REITA. Just before I bought the salon.

KAMAL. You came to my Auntieji's house, three a.m., my wedding morning. Like a doctor, carrying your red make-up case. Photo of a beauty queen stuck inside.

> (**REITA** *stops.*)

Said your Mummyji gave it to you.

> (**REITA** *nods.*)

I watched you in the mirror. Making me blossom in the dawn light. Twisting my hair up into a bun, painting my bridal face, sliding a tikka through my hair, a nath through my nose. Dressing me in my red blouse and lengha – gold sequins, a thousand rising suns. Remember?

REITA. *(Resumes the manicure.)* I've made up so many brides...

KAMAL. Home alone, I flick through the wedding album, wishing I could be as hopeful as back then.

REITA. When the make-up and mehndi fades, wedding party's over. Real married life begins!

KAMAL. I want to feel beautiful again. As beautiful as you made me feel that day.

> (**REITA** *pulls up* **KAMAL**'s *sleeve slightly to start painting her nails.*)

REITA. Hai, what did you do here?

KAMAL. *(Pulling her sleeve back down.)* My little girl.

REITA. Sharp nails.

KAMAL. She loves walking all over me. Like we would walk and fall all over our Mummyjis...?

REITA. Our feet pushing out a laugh around her bottom –

KAMAL. A "hai" scream on her back –

TANWANT. *(Coming out of the cubicle.)* "Luchi-kuthi-kamini-haramjadi-randi", when you climbed on her shoulders!

> *(The women laugh.)*

REITA. My daughter loves walking all over me too.

KAMAL. How old is she?

REITA. Teenage handful. Fifteen.

KAMAL. A child.

REITA. When I was fifteen, I believed everything my Dad told me. Never questioned him. Now, our children tell us what to do, question everything we say.

KAMAL. At fifteen, I knew nothing. Now I know things I wish I'd never seen or felt...

> *(**PINKY** bursts into the salon, carrying a huge accessory bag. She wears heavy make up, sunglasses, a glittery top and tight jeans under a big coat, wet from the rain.)*

PINKY. Man, you see what's goin' on outside?

> *(**PINKY** takes off her sunglasses, hurling her wet coat and bag over the chairs. **REITA** picks up after **PINKY**.)*

TANWANT. What happen out there?

REITA. Pinky, work experience means arriving at work on time.

PINKY. Couldn't get past the Feds –

TANWANT. Fed? How many Fed?

PINKY. They're all over yeah! Got tape all over! Couldn't get past. Wouldn't let me past. Fucking Feds. Fucking hate the Feds!

REITA. *(To* **PINKY.***)* Language. *(Turning back, resuming the manicure.)* Sorry Kamal.

PINKY. *Fucking* Feds blocked off the road – and the station.

REITA. Pinky.

TANWANT. *(To* **PINKY.***)* Why? Kamali know nothing.

PINKY. Another one under –

TANWANT. One undie? What it is?

PINKY. When someone jumps in front of a train, dies under –

TANWANT. Ho Waheguru.

REITA. Talk about something else.

PINKY. When you got to take the train, you think Freshie tart, thanks for the delays.

REITA. *(To* **PINKY.***)* Where do you take the train?

>   *(***PINKY*** *ignores* **REITA.***)*

TANWANT. Hai, what bout poor driver? He see woman jump. See bloody inside spill outside – skin, flesh, organ, like atta, stick to black iron track...

KAMAL. *(Getting up.)* I – I got to go –

REITA. But – I haven't finished –

>   *(***KAMAL*** *rushes out of the salon.)*

REITA. *(Shouting after **KAMAL**.)* Let your nails... dry!

PINKY. Such. A. Weirdo.

> *(**TANWANT** nods in agreement. **REITA** clears the table.)*

*(To **REITA**.)* Seriously, why you so nice to her?

> *(**REITA** heads into a cubicle and streams relaxing Indian music* through the salon.)*

Just cos some saddo tart don't want to live, don't mean the rest of us don't.

TANWANT. *(Nodding.)* Haan, selfish...

PINKY. Selfish, cos once they're dead, why still hang round?

TANWANT. What you mean?

PINKY. Someone said after those women kill themselves, their spirits drift by the tracks, in white shalwar kameezes – or white saris –

TANWANT. Sari more nice, hunnah?

PINKY. Then their spirits suddenly appear up on the road, flag down a male driver. Sometimes, the women talk. Sometimes, they don't. Sometimes, their faces are all mashed up with blood and scars. Even if the shook driver tries speeding away, the women just slide right through the door, into the back of the car! Then, when the driver looks in the rear-view mirror – there's no-one there.

TANWANT. *(Shivers.)* Nahi.

> *(**PINKY** nods.)*

---

* A licence to produce LOTUS BEAUTY does not include a performance licence for any third-party or copyrighted music. Licensees should create an original composition or use music in the public domain. For further information, please see Music Use Note on page iii.

Waheguru. *(Shivers.)* So, what else you know bout this one?

PINKY. Nuffin' else. Feds kept us well away from da crime scene.

> *(**REITA** heads back out of the cubicle.)*

Then the train track crackheads started chatting me up –

REITA. I've told you to keep away from there.

> *(The desk phone rings. **TANWANT** answers the phone, speaking in muted tones.)*

PINKY. Just cos you're too shit scared to go there, don't mean I can't.

> *(**REITA** takes cleaning products from the desk. She holds them out for **PINKY**.)*

REITA. Clean and polish the mirrors and surfaces. Floor needs a sweep too.

PINKY. Get your Freshie cleaner to do it.

REITA. I want the cleaning done.

PINKY. She's your cleaner. I'm your daughter.

REITA. You're on work experience – so experience doing some work.

PINKY. I would if you had any clients.

REITA. Beauty isn't just about make-up and dress up.

PINKY. *(Mock horror.)* You lied to me all these years?

REITA. To know beauty, you need to know the ugly bits too.

PINKY. I just walked past an ugly suicide scene. Need to chill, find the beauty again.

(REITA puts down the products next to PINKY and heads into the cubicle. PINKY takes selfies in various poses, as TANWANT finishes the call.)

TANWANT. *(Hanging up.)* Ok theek ya, bye!

PINKY. Something well dark must have happened in that woman's life.

TANWANT. Why you no this interest in schoolwork?

PINKY. S'not real life innit? Wanna see life through my phone, as it happens. Not through some crappy past it textbook. *(Proudly.)* Tej taught me that.

TANWANT. Education passport to proper life. You paagal throw away like this.

PINKY. Not when I got this business to fall back on.

TANWANT. Only with proper skill, proper qualification. Tear off client skin with wax, burn skin with laser – skill in torture camp – not *Lotus Beauty* salon.

PINKY. Who said I'd do any work? You'll all be doing it for me.

TANWANT. Sachi?

PINKY. *(Taking a selfie.)* Cos I'll be too busy getting famous.

TANWANT. As what?

PINKY. Ain't worked that out yet.

TANWANT. I think I be famous when young. Now, I pray no-one recognise me. *(Her phone beeps. She checks.)* Bloody hell. Nother jection from Shaadi website. *(Flings her phone aside.)*

PINKY. *(Checking her selfies.)* Tanni, thread my eyebrows.

TANWANT. I waiting client. She on Punjabi time 'gain.

PINKY. You're the best threader in da ghetto West.

TANWANT. *(Flattered.)* Blesses you.

PINKY. Should grab you when I can. Learn from the master.

TANWANT. *(Getting up.)* Ok, jaldi, before she turn up.

> (**PINKY** *rushes to the chair by the manicure table.* **TANWANT** *grabs a roll of thread and breaks off a long piece.* **PINKY** *types away on her phone.*)

(Demonstrating.) Break long thread. Loop round finger. Make scissor thread. Line up hair. Catch hair in scissor thread... Oi, you listen?

PINKY. *(Typing on her phone.)* I'm listening.

TANWANT. Slide like this... pluck hair as you go. *(In sweeping rhythm.)* Like apnay boys mowing grass outside my five star garden flat, where your Mummyji say rent so low...

> (**TANWANT** *threads* **PINKY**'s *eyebrows, losing herself in a threading groove.*)

Gal sun, you know your special new friend?

PINKY. Intimately.

TANWANT. Hai, I no want to know... you say he help...

PINKY. *(Stops messaging.)* He always helps...

TANWANT. *(Taps* **PINKY**'s *eyebrow.)* Stretch.

PINKY. That's what he likes to say.

> (**TANWANT** *mock slaps* **PINKY**, *who giggles.*)

TANWANT. So he help?

PINKY. You know the deal. He'll find you a husband so quick. Then you'll owe him – and me.

TANWANT. I already cover you for school.

PINKY. Doesn't even begin to cover it.

TANWANT. Your mum find out, she rip off my skin, then fire me live!

PINKY. Cos she'd step away from her life for one second, see what's goin' on in mine?

TANWANT. Nahi, I no sure...

PINKY. Drag your chappals, he'll change his mind.

TANWANT. Oh Pinky...

> (**REITA** *heads out of the cubicle, typing on her phone and sees* **TANWANT** *threading.*)

REITA. *(To* **TANWANT.***)* Why aren't you doing a Pampering Package on Sangeeta?

TANWANT. She no turn up yet.

> (**PINKY** *gets up to check her eyebrows in the mirror.*)

REITA. Again?

TANWANT. No phone. Nothing. I leave her three message.

REITA. Message her back and charge her for not giving 24 hours notice. If I'd charged her for all her missed appointments, I could have bought my new house and salon by now – in cash. Seriously, the women round here, booking, then not showing up –

> (**TANWANT** *types on her phone.* **PINKY** *spots something sticking out behind the mirror.*)

PINKY. Hey, what's this behind the...?

> (**PINKY** *pulls out a dusty black and white photograph and blows off the dust.*)

TANWANT. What it is?

(**REITA** *takes the photo and wipes the plastic clean.* **TANWANT** *peers over.*)

REITA. Oh God.

PINKY. Who that?

TANWANT. *(To* **REITA**.*)* Your Mummyji? She Miss World?

REITA. No, no, it's Reita –

PINKY. You? Miss World? Say Mums!

REITA. Not me! Reita Faria.

PINKY. Who?

TANWANT. Why she hide behind your mirror?

REITA. *(Staring.)* Must have stuck her there, when I opened the salon...

PINKY. Check out her bling bling crown! Her Indian beehive!

REITA. It's from London, 1966.

PINKY. My Angrez brothers still bang on like all the goras bout 1966. England blah blah won the World Cup blah blah –

REITA. – and India won Miss World. First time.

TANWANT. Ohhhh. I no see her before. I know only 1994. When Ash and Sush went pretty head to head for Miss India. No pull apart with swimming costume. So big shock when Sush beat Ash. Sush win Miss India, then Miss Universe. But Ash win Miss World. India dil went so paagal! We womans cake face in make-up, rub this cream, that cream. Look in mirror, see Miss India, Miss World, Miss Universe smile back. Nuclear superpower be beauty superpower. India had beauty and nuclear bomb. First time world see us as beautiful – really beautiful.

REITA. Mum named me after her.

TANWANT. Ohhhh, when I first see R.E.I.T.A., I think Reita just being gori gori again!

REITA. Dad was angry I wasn't a boy –

PINKY. Like you were, when you saw I was a girl?

REITA. Mum said she was drying my tears as a baby, when she looked down on the dusty ground. An Indian Queen was looking up at her, wearing a crown, gown, radiant smile. Mum tore out the picture, wrapped it in plastic. I found it in her suitcase – the one she never had strength to pack.

PINKY. What happened to your mum?

REITA. I'm her age now. *(To* **PINKY.***)* Your age when she died.

PINKY. *You* – a teenager?

REITA. A teenager who wore wide flapping shalwar kameezes to school, two plaits, greased down with a thick Indian accent –

PINKY. *(Laughing.)* An original Freshie?

REITA. Plaits like tentacles growing out of my head. The English girls would pull me into their skipping circle. One girl would grab one plait. Another girl would grab the other. Never held my hands. "A ring a ring o' roses/A pocket full o' poesies". "Atishoo, atishoo!" Then they'd all spin me round. Push me to the ground. "We all fall down". Spit on me. When I got home, mum would wipe my tears. Show me this photo. "Your name is Reita".

TANWANT. Wish my Mummyji had wipe my tears when I little.

PINKY. Mine too.

*(***REITA** *continues staring at the photo.)*

TANWANT. When I little, I always think one day, ehna sohna husband will find me, look after me with his big heart, big wallet. I start so well. Thusi mainu believe nahi karenge but when I eighteen, I has brain *and* beauty – I win 'Miss Punjab'!

REITA. You?

TANWANT. Haan. *Me.*

PINKY. *(Laughing.)* You in a teeny weeny sexy Reita Faria bikini?

TANWANT. Is Punjab stupid. Womans cover up, not strip off. For 'Miss Punjab' Household Round, I wear heavy shalwar kameez and do chakki – grind the corn!

REITA. You ground corn... in a beauty contest?

TANWANT. A-ho! Got points for how well I grind it! I top the table! In Bridal Round, I model wife. Peep from behind five stone dupatta, like my real wedding. In Talent Round, I do giddha like my wedding dance –

>   (**TANWANT** *giddha dances around the manicure table.* **REITA** *and* **PINKY** *laugh.*)

(Slumps back in chair.) Chak de phatte I village catch! Mummyji even frame my 'Miss Punjab' photo. She so proud, she pass it round with her best chaa and barfi. So many sticky fingerprint... before she smash it into chhote piece –

PINKY. What did you do?

>   *(Pause.)*

TANWANT. *(Teary.)* I – I with the baby.

REITA/PINKY. What?

>   (**TANWANT** *nods.*)

TANWANT. Then boy I love, run from village.

PINKY. Why?

TANWANT. Muslim.

PINKY.	REITA.
Hell nah!/	Oh.

> *(Pause.)*

REITA. Your baby?

TANWANT. Girl. How I keep?

REITA. You got rid of her?

TANWANT. Single mother? Unmarried? Muslim-Sikh baby? Punjab?

REITA. Oh Tanni.

TANWANT. Better I rot here, than her and me there.

PINKY. Yeah, mos def much better here. Two girls in my year got pregnant –

REITA. Your age?

PINKY. But lucky, both did a foetus-deletus. Families never found out.

> *(**REITA** shakes her head.)*

TANWANT. Meri kismet, all gossipy village find out.

REITA. This town isn't any different.

> *(**REITA** puts the photograph on the desk, checks her phone and heads into the kitchen. Sniffling, **TANWANT** composes herself. **PINKY** checks her face in the mirror.)*

PINKY. Wanna talk about it?

> *(**TANWANT** shakes her head stoically.)*

Finish my other eyebrow then?

(Shaking her head, **TANWANT** *begins threading* **PINKY***'s eyebrows, as* **BIG DHADHI** *hobbles into the Salon on her walking stick, carrying a blue plastic bag of fruit. She has a long white beard and wears a wet anorak over her shalwar kameez.)*

TANWANT. Haaah, BD! Quick!

*(***TANWANT*** and* **PINKY** *break off from threading.* **PINKY** *runs towards* **BIG DHADHI***, smothering her in kisses.)*

Sat Sri Akal BD!

BIG DHADHI. Where she is?

*(***PINKY*** points to the cubicle and* **TANWANT** *helps* **BIG DHADHI** *take off her anorak.)*

Push push. Dhakkay maardi saraa dhin. 'When Harmeet and boys leave house, you leave house'. Big dhakka push in road, rain –

PINKY. *(Leads* **BIG DHADHI** *to a chair.)* Aaja BD, thora raam kar.

BIG DHADHI. I clean airport thirty year. Thirty year! Wipe floor, fingerprint, handprint, shoe print, sweep dirt, pick litter, clean ehnay gunday toilet. Thirty year I work for my house. And she take my key? When Waheguru *(Points to the sky.)* call me, he give real key. No her.

PINKY. Big Dhari – Big Dhadhi, your dhari? *(Strokes* **BIG DHADHI***'s beard.)* Is it longer?

BIG DHADHI. *(Slaps away* **PINKY***'s hand.)* If Waheguru make beard grow to earth, so be. He make beard scatter on earth, so be. He say, "Time for go", I go. He say, "stay", I stay. But some days, main tuhanu dassdi, I ready to go.

PINKY. I'll trim it first, smooth on some wax, then rip it off yeah?

BIG DHADHI. Shittari di kachi!

> (**BIG DHADHI** *struggles onto a chair.* **PINKY** *sits at reception, playing on her phone. The phone rings, which* **PINKY** *ignores. Rolling her eyes at* **PINKY,** **TANWANT** *answers.*)

Bone thap, body snap, arthrighty jab, hai mere godhay... *(Presses her knees.)* Knees crack like earth I run on so fast as little girl. Still, she dhakka push push saraa dhin.

> (**REITA** *heads back with a cup of tea.*)

REITA. *(To* **BIG DHADHI.***)* You're here?

BIG DHADHI. *(Trying to get up.)* Haan, want me to go? Want my pension book?

REITA. Not now BD.

BIG DHADHI. Not now? *(Hurls her pension book to the floor.)* Here! Lehjaa! He will give me real key, real pension – no you!

> (**TANWANT** *finishes the phone call.*)

REITA. *(Pocketing the pension book.)* We should all pay our way. Even Pinky's working here – for free.

BIG DHADHI. Ki? I no pay?

REITA. Bas. I've got clients coming in a few minutes.

BIG DHADHI. Then look after them. 'Cos you has one less client out there.

REITA. What?

> (**PINKY** *and* **TANWANT** *look quizzically at each other.*)

BIG DHADHI. Suicide.

PINKY. Train track?

BIG DHADHI. Haan. *(To* **REITA.***)* One of your.

> *(***TANWANT,   REITA** *and* **PINKY** *exchange shocked glances.)*

TANWANT. Who?

BIG DHADHI. No name –

PINKY. – yet. BD CID needs more time.

BIG DHADHI. "Auntieji, she go *Reita* salon".

TANWANT. *(To* **REITA.***)* Who could be?

BIG DHADHI. Someone say husband live on…

PINKY. Where BD?

BIG DHADHI. … Burns Avenue.

> *(***REITA** *and* **TANWANT** *gasp.)*

REITA/TANWANT. *(Shocked, to each other.)* Sangeeta.

REITA. No.

TANWANT. She just miss her Pamper Package.

PINKY. Hard to make if you're dead.

TANWANT. Why she kill herself?

BIG DHADHI. *(To* **REITA.***)* You know?

REITA. How would I know?

PINKY. You know BD?

BIG DHADHI. *(Eyeing* **REITA.***)* Haan, I know.

TANWANT. Why BD?

BIG DHADHI. She do puthe kam.

PINKY. What bad thing?

BIG DHADHI. Puthe kam gainst husband.

REITA. But she only got married recently.

TANWANT. *(To* **REITA.***)* Husband was from there, hunnah?

PINKY. O-oh.

BIG DHADHI. "O-oh" di lagdi. I find you sachi nice boy from there. Big turban, big beard, baptise, ehna handsome. No your Mummyji. Me.

PINKY. *(Slathering on red lipstick.)* Not if I find someone first.

REITA. *(To* **TANWANT.***)* Didn't he go back after the wedding? To wait for his papers?

TANWANT. Haan. Sangeeta tell me when she last here for full body wax. She spend half hour taking off wedding bangle after bangle –

BIG DHADHI. *(Shaking her head.)* Paagal womans! Never take off wedding bangle.

PINKY. Why? Cos they're like kinky handcuffs?

(**REITA** *glares at* **PINKY.***)*

TANWANT. New bride s'pose to wait for every bangle to smash in passion on marriage bed –

PINKY. "Passion?" With bits of glass stuck in your arse?

BIG DHADHI. *(Eyeing* **REITA.***)* Reita bangle never smash. I has to rub oil on her puffy hand, pull off bangle, one by one. All my bangle smash one day.

TANWANT. Rabba, hope mine smash quick as well.

REITA. *(To* **TANWANT,** *pointing to the cubicle.)* Did you fix the machine in there?

(**TANWANT** *reluctantly saunters to the cubicle, leaving the door open.)*

(To **BIG DHADHI.***)* What else do you know?

(**BIG DHADHI** *remains silent.*)

PINKY. BD!

BIG DHADHI. She five month with baby.

(**TANWANT** *gasps in the cubicle doorway.*)

PINKY. She killed her unborn baby?

TANWANT. And his.

BIG DHADHI. Nahi. *(Pause.)* Baby not his.

(**TANWANT** *and* **PINKY** *gasp.*)

TANWANT. Whose it was?

BIG DHADHI. Eh ni mainu pata. But husband only pakka permanent UK one month go.

PINKY. Then he should have got here sooner innit?

BIG DHADHI. She five month with baby by then.

PINKY. Why leave her on her own for so long?

BIG DHADHI. So long? When your Big Dhadha come UK, I stay in Punjab seven year – seven year – without him. Then I follow.

PINKY. No naughty village business for you then BD?

BIG DHADHI. Sharam kar.

TANWANT. Sangeeta was so happy, so chatty. Big Hema Malini eyes, lotus pink cheek, bee sting lip. Reita make her so beautiful on wedding day... you see her body BD?

BIG DHADHI. Nahi. But I see husband.

TANWANT. Haah, where?

BIG DHADHI. Outside station.

REITA. How was he?

BIG DHADHI. Chaukaree cross leg on pavement, hand full ehna khoon and tears.

REITA. Her blood.

TANWANT. So sad for him.

PINKY. "Sad for him?" What bout her?

TANWANT. She dead now. He still live.

> (**REITA** *points* **TANWANT** *to the cubicle. She heads in.*)

BIG DHADHI. *(Glares at **REITA**.)* All has to go sometime. Coat ready, suitcase pack.

PINKY. *(To **REITA**.)* You didn't know, bout the other man?

REITA. How? Women come, women go. We pamper them, preen them, make them beautiful. Make small talk. Never know what's really under their skin. Poor Sangeeta.

BIG DHADHI. Bahuth vadi bechari! Someone else baby? He must has big shock. Big shock.

REITA. Big shock because he couldn't be here –

TANWANT. *(From doorway.)* – if no papers.

BIG DHADHI. Then why marry if she no wait him?

TANWANT. She seem happy for marry and wait.

PINKY. Lover boy was clearly too smokin' …

BIG DHADHI. What woman this is? Ruin her life, husband life, baby life.

TANWANT. No on purpose BD.

BIG DHADHI. Life precious gift from Waheguru. We has to live with all dukh-sukh life give us. No throw our life, other people life when too hard.

PINKY. Don't worry, I mos def gonna make the most of my life.

BIG DHADHI. Or even if she suffer with husband, stay live, show him – no kill him too!

REITA. Not if she couldn't go on.

BIG DHADHI. This how us womans survive – be strong.

REITA. We're not all as strong as you BD.

BIG DHADHI. No always do what you want. Gal sundi aa? Think bout husband, children, family... no always do you what you want. Gal sundi aa?

(A high-speed train races by in the distance.)

REITA. I hear. I hear. *(Pause.)* And I've had enough. Soon as I can, I'm out of this dead-end town.

ACT TWO

Bud

(Next day. Lunch. **REITA** *works on a client in a screened cubicle. Low-level Punjabi music* fills the salon.* **TANWANT** *waves off a client at the door.)*

TANWANT. See you next week Meena! *(Lamenting, closing the door.)* How she get sachi handsome husband, hain?

(The desk phone rings.)

(Answers the phone.) Good Afternoon Lotus Beauty... Hello?.. Hello? *(Lowers tone.)* You no sharam?... not even do scary breath proper? Do like this. *(Breathes with attempted menace.)*... stop pester me!... or next time, I scream so loud, your wife or China lodger girl hear me!

*(***REITA*** slips out of the cubicle, making a call.)*

Haan, you wife here now. Want talk her? *(Slams down phone, cursing "Haramjada" under her breath.)*

REITA. Harmeet is –

TANWANT. He call me Reita.

---

* A licence to produce LOTUS BEAUTY does not include a performance licence for any third-party or copyrighted music. Licensees should create an original composition or use music in the public domain. For further information, please see Music Use Note on page iii.

REITA. *(Stops.)* Who?

TANWANT. Man... who want... strip... wax. I tell him we ladies only.

REITA. *(Ignoring* **TANWANT**, *hanging up.)* Harmeet's busy on his phone, again.

TANWANT. Cos he always on it... finding job.

REITA. *(Scrolling on her phone.)* Here – one of Councillor Gill's seven houses up for sale.

TANWANT. Rabba, seven? She buy house like I buy lipstick.

REITA. *(Showing the photos.)* Perfect isn't it? Green, leafy town next door. Big white house. Tall, gold-topped iron gates. Paved driveway for five cars. Stately columns propping up the front porch. Conservatory, tiled patio, huge garden, out back. Extension to the back and sides, loft room up top, five bedrooms, ensuite bathrooms, separate rooms for Harmeet and me –

TANWANT. Shed too?

REITA. Spacious one I can rent out for more.

TANWANT. More?

REITA. *(Showing more photos.)* And this – the salon space.

TANWANT. In shopping centre?

REITA. Next to one. Councillor sells to me, she's got my vote.

TANWANT. But Reita, what I will –?

REITA. I'm meeting her soon, to see both. Might even put in an offer –

TANWANT. Today?

REITA. Then soon as I can afford, a deposit –

TANWANT. Deposit? Sperm or egg bank? Cos I be thinking – /

REITA. *(Looking at the photos.)* – if both are as perfect as they look.

TANWANT. So, you sell BD's house?

REITA. *My* house.

TANWANT. But this 'dead' Southall, peoples know people, peoples help people – and your beautiful house right now, I dream to live there…

REITA. That house is like this saggy skin – doesn't fit anymore. Ugh, that seventies jungli wallpaper she won't let me tear down. Those plants will grow out the walls and throttle me –

TANWANT. – live in shed where real plant grow out of wall, throttle me.

REITA. Should have rented a more expensive room inside, like the Chinese lodgers.

TANWANT. BD has all thing in 'dead' town – gurdwara, fruit shop, sabji shop, gossip stop – all in Punjabi.

REITA. She needs to learn English properly.

TANWANT. Her age?

REITA. Stretch more than her gossip muscles.

TANWANT. All peoples like her speak Punjabi here.

REITA. We live in England.

TANWANT. She might get lost, not walk so well in leafy town –

REITA. Don't let that walking stick fool you.

TANWANT. She'd rest knees at home all time if you let her.

REITA. Home alone, she'd burn my house down. Or flood it.

TANWANT. Pinky got school here.

REITA. Finishes next summer. We'll be closer to a good college, away from train track druggies, drunks, wasters, knocked up teens –

TANWANT. They happy to move?

REITA. Harmeet will talk to BD. Not a word 'til then. I'll talk to Pinky over lunch and the boys tonight. Once we move, I'll get my face and body done too –

TANWANT. We no be happy with what we got?

REITA. Are you?

>   (*The desk phone rings.* REITA *heads into the empty cubicle, dialling on her phone.*)

TANWANT. (*Angrily.*) What I say hain? (*Changing her tone.*) Oh Dolly! Where you be hiding?… Achaa?… *You* find nice husband? Oh… vadhaiyan! Hope for all us singly woman then innit?… Any left?… Now you got husband, no more hide jungli arms and legs under big kameez tent! Or you no scuse if husband run after fresh pluck duckie for a quick fuckie – ahem… Haan, meri kismet, still looking…

>   (**PINKY** *comes back in, chooses a nail varnish bottle from the shelf.*)

Haan… so what you want? (*Writes.*) One three-quarter leg, two full arm, one underarm. When?… Haan, I can do… OK, see any man for me, call ek dhum, theek ya? (*Puts down phone. To* **PINKY**.) Your mum serious about house move.

PINKY. And I'm serious about getting even more hot 'n' heavy with Tej.

TANWANT. What I do hain?

PINKY. Stop stalking sad shaadi sites and listen to me – Tej will help you.

>   (**PINKY** *sits down, begins painting her nails.*)

TANWANT. Pinky, am I pashoo in the pind?

PINKY. You what?

TANWANT. In Punjab, everyone got shed in courtyard. Cattle sleep there, eat there, do toilet there, be push round there –

PINKY. Least you got a shed. Other day, me and Tej saw this sad Freshie fall out a filthy wheelie bin. Tej said the Freshie's sleeping in there. Man, we laughed so hard.

TANWANT. Sharam kar, why you call us that?

PINKY. *(Holds up a bottle.)* Think this colour suits me?

TANWANT. *(Praying with folded hands.)* Waheguru, please, ek husband ek dhum.

PINKY. This one's better... nah, this one... *(Holds up two bottles.)* Ahhh, which one?

> *(**REITA** emerges from the cubicle.)*

REITA. Where's BD?

PINKY. Slid into the toilet, climbing out using her beard as a rope?

REITA. When she's out, tell her to go home. Your dad's waiting – for his roti.

> *(**PINKY** rolls her eyes.)*

And Tanni, Harmeet says your rent is late – again.

TANWANT. Last night, he say pay when I can.

REITA. New house, new salon...

> *(**PINKY** scoffs.)*

I can take it from next month's pay.

TANWANT. What I left to eat with?

REITA. Whatever's left over.

TANWANT. I already pay below minimum wage –

REITA. Cash in hand, tax free –

TANWANT. Sorry. I pay soon.

PINKY. For such a crummy little shed?

REITA. *(To* **TANWANT.***)* It's a sweet garden flat isn't it?

TANWANT. Hanji.

PINKY. *(To* **REITA.***)* I used to hide in that dump from you.

REITA. *(To* **PINKY.***)* Did you?

PINKY. First time when I started my period. Blood had soaked through my knickers, skirt, onto the chair in class –

TANWANT. Hai.

REITA. TMI.

PINKY. No info from you about what was happening. I hid in that shed for hours.

REITA. Well, your old hiding place is all spruced up now for Tanni to enjoy.

PINKY. I can still see the stains.

REITA. *(To* **TANWANT.***)* We're waiting…

> (**REITA** *heads back to her client in the cubicle.*
> **TANWANT** *speaks in conspiratorial tones so*
> **REITA** *does not hear.)*

TANWANT. OK, cancel Bollywood romance. I take any husband. Need your help.

PINKY. Cool, you owe me.

TANWANT. You no do anything yet.

PINKY. *(Holding up her phone.)* I'll do it right now –

TANWANT. He help, even if I earn roti crumb?

PINKY. Tej will make you a fake identity for a big loan you take out. Cleared by a bank insider. Tej gets a big cut cos he's doing most of the work and you, a tiny one.

> (**REITA** *comes out to collect treatment items, a couple of times.* **TANWANT** *and* **PINKY** *break off their conversation, resuming when* **REITA** *heads back into the cubicle.*)

TANWANT. Police really come after me then, isn't it?

PINKY. Chill. You won't exist, so they won't. Everyone scams. Legals, illegals, the government, even the banks. They get away with it. Why not you?

TANWANT. On road, I bow head, so I no see police. When cubicle shake, I think is police? Look at client, think, she undercover police? Limbo life. So many mundey, khuriya go back, cos they no work, no money, no place to live here. Even if I has nothing, how I go back to Mummyji? My village? How I go back after many month, money, mountain, desert, forest, boat, lorry, to reach here?

PINKY. Say yes. Tej says "say yes". We're only thinking of you. Here's his number. *(Taps on her phone.)* You see, Tej is a mover and shaker, not a waster.

TANWANT. *(Picking up* **PINKY**'s *pinging message.)* No husband material either.

PINKY. Nah, he's so peng, tattooed, model rippingly fit. Hero material.

TANWANT. You never think be careful?

PINKY. For being in love?

TANWANT. You even know what is love?

PINKY. Tej gives me everything I need. Things I don't even realise I need.

TANWANT. Gal sun, love is like butter. We think cos butter smooth skin, it good nuff to eat. So we eat big, hungry mouthful. Then, it clog you up, break your heart. This why so many heart-attack Punjabi. Actually, I hungry for butter chaupri roti right now. Pinky, you too young. See what happen me.

PINKY. *(Pointing at* TANWANT*'s phone.)* Text, before he switches numbers.

> *(*REITA *comes out to collect more items.* PINKY *quickly resumes painting her nails and* TANWANT *reluctantly texts.)*

REITA. *What* are you two doing?

TANWANT. *(Pointing to the empty cubicle.)* I get cubicle ready for Naz – Pinky help me...

REITA. Out here, on your phone?

TANWANT. I... I...text... Sangeeta. Too sad do in same cubicle I pamper her last.

REITA. Sangeeta?

TANWANT. Feel bad... so I... I leave her message.

REITA. But she's dead.

TANWANT. Yesterday, I leave message charging her for no cancellation notice –

REITA. You didn't...

TANWANT. You tell me. So now I say ok she not come. We no charge her. *(Presses 'Send'.)* There I send. Waheguru.

> *(*BIG DHADHI *hobbles back.)*

REITA. She must have felt so lost.

TANWANT. We only see people from outside. Who know what happen inside?

PINKY. Thought you'd slipped into the toilet BD.

BIG DHADHI. Puth, no move fast as I use to.

REITA. *(Gathering treatment items, to* **BIG DHADHI.***)* You need to go home.

> *(***BIG DHADHI** *ignores* **REITA.** *Her kameez is stuck in her shalwar.* **REITA** *notices it, shakes her head.* **TANWANT** *pulls out the kameez from* **BIG DHADHI***'s shalwar.* **BIG DHADHI** *sits down, eating an orange she picks out of her carrier bag.)*

BD?

BIG DHADHI. Better we burn our peoples. All this gora hocus pocus – bury in box, bury in ground. Nothing left but chhil shell. Like peel without fruit. Pinky –

> *(***BIG DHADHI** *holds out the peel for* **PINKY,** *who annoyed and painting her nails, takes the peel and trying to avoid ruining her wet nails, misses the dustbin. She heads back to the desk, to continue doing her nails.* **TANWANT** *picks up the peel and throws it into the dustbin. She heads in and out of the cubicle.* **BIG DHADHI** *eats her orange, looking down at her feet.)*

REITA. *(To* **BIG DHADHI.***)* You need to go home. Now.

BIG DHADHI. Go, stay, go, stay – I no traffic light Reita.

REITA. Harmeet is waiting for his roti.

BIG DHADHI. Cut my toe-nail. Then I go.

REITA. I'm working.

BIG DHADHI. Nail poke out of shoe, feet hurt when walk. Aaja.

REITA. Pinky, cut your grandmother's toe-nails.

PINKY. *(Not looking up.)* She asked you –

REITA. – and I'm telling you.

PINKY. I ain't cutting her toe-nails yeah?

REITA. It's work experience.

PINKY. More like a scarring experience.

REITA. I've got a client in there, a meeting after lunch and BD needs to make your Dad's lunch. Cut them.

PINKY. When do you ever care if he eats lunch or not?

REITA. *(Picking up the desk phone.)* Shall I call your school to find you other work experience?

PINKY. *(Reaching over, stopping* REITA.*)* No, no, don't – do that.

> (**REITA** *picks up a large nail clipper and holds it out, which* **PINKY** *snatches.)*

REITA. Quickly, please.

> (**REITA** *heads back into the cubicle with a bowl of items.)*

PINKY. I ain't doin' it. *(Holds out the clipper for* **TANWANT**.*)* You do it.

TANWANT. She your Grand-Mums.

PINKY. One day, I'll run this Salon. Best you listen to me now.

TANWANT. I run my Salon by then, with gori gori skin bed for dark ladies in one cubicle, suntan bed for gori ladies in other cubicle... You no boss yet. Your Mum is, so I tell her if you no cut BD toe-nail.

PINKY. You owe me.

TANWANT. When he make something happen.

PINKY. *(Annoyed, hobbling to* **BIG DHADHI**.*)* Ugh! BD, a tenner to cut your toe-nails.

BIG DHADHI. *(Trying to pull off a sock.)* Hain puth?

TANWANT. *(To* **PINKY.***)* Thori sharam kar!

> *(***PINKY** *reluctantly sits at* **BIG DHADHI***'s feet.)*

In India, cutting grandparent toe-nail is big honour.

> *(***BIG DHADHI** *triumphantly pulls off one of her socks.)*

PINKY. Honour? Seen the state of 'em?

BIG DHADHI. *(Blesses* **PINKY**, *touching her head.)* Saadi Pinky, sachi ehni good girl.

PINKY. Don't mess up the hair BD!

> *(***PINKY** *struggles to clip a big toe-nail, watches it fly and land by* **TANWANT**, *who picks it up.)*

TANWANT. *(Holding up the nail.)* Calceem from gurdwara chaa and kheer, hunnah BD?

> *(***BIG DHADHI** *stares vacantly ahead.)*

PINKY. *(To* **BIG DHADHI***.)* You chattin' to Waheguru again?

BIG DHADHI. That poor husband. Bechara.

PINKY. Omg! What about Sangeeta?

BIG DHADHI. He has nothing. No-one here.

TANWANT. More worse – now she dead, what if he sent back?

BIG DHADHI. *(Nods.)* Sahi gal.

TANWANT. When he marry her, he think he pakka in UK for life.

BIG DHADHI. His family all there. Who s'port him here?

PINKY. You can. You can chat to him bout Waheguru and he can cut your toe-nails.

BIG DHADHI. Wife no even here for him.

PINKY. Cos she killed herself BD.

BIG DHADHI. He just sit on dirty road, all lone. All lone.

TANWANT. Maybe someone will visit from India, to s'port him.

BIG DHADHI. Who from there, come all way here?

PINKY. Oh, someone will come. Getting them back might be the problem.

> (**BIG DHADHI** *raises her chunni over her head and recites a Waheguru refrain, using her Sikh mala beads.* **REITA** *brings out a client, says goodbye and turns the sign from 'Open to Closed'. Walking in and out,* **TANWANT** *cleans up her cubicle and prepares for her afternoon clients.*)

REITA. *(To* **PINKY.***)* You done?

PINKY. Clipping stone age toenails?

REITA. Clip quickly for now. Finish them later.

PINKY. "Quickly?" If you've got a chainsaw –

REITA. *(To* **BIG DHADHI.***)* Your puthar son is getting impatient.

BIG DHADHI. "My puthar son"? *Your* husband.

REITA. He's hungry. Really hungry.

PINKY. I'll call him, tell him to get take out – as usual.

REITA. BD needs to eat too.

PINKY. Care today do you?

BIG DHADHI. Ajj, we all eat here, together.

TANWANT. Haan BD! We get chupri lunch from Kulcha Cottage. I pick up –

REITA. He wants his Mummyji's roti, today.

BIG DHADHI. Give me key.

REITA. He'll be home.

BIG DHADHI. When he out all time?

REITA. He'll be there, waiting.

BIG DHADHI. Dhakkay here, dhakkay there but no key.

PINKY. BD, I'll walk you home.

REITA. *(To* **PINKY.***)* No, I need to talk to you over lunch.

PINKY. *(Finishing, to* **BIG DHADHI.***)* There, thank Waheguru, cutting khatam, done.

BIG DHADHI. *(Looking at her toes.)* Still poke –

REITA. They're fine.

PINKY. *(Offering* **BIG DHADHI** *the nail cuttings on a tissue.)* Want these to slice up your fruit and sabjis?

> *(***REITA** *grabs the tissue of nails and throws it away.)*

REITA. *(To* **BIG DHADHI.***)* Home please.

BIG DHADHI. *(Pressing her knees.)* Need to napp my godhay –

PINKY. *(Starts pressing* **BIG DHADHI***'s knees.)* Let her rest.

REITA. *(Urging* **BIG DHADHI.***)* Up.

BIG DHADHI. *(Rising.)* Pinky, chadd. Big boss no hear no one pain – no even her own.

> *(Shooting cutting looks at* **REITA**, **PINKY** *helps* **BIG DHADHI** *to the door. She kisses* **BIG DHADHI** *goodbye. As* **BIG DHADHI** *walks out, slamming the door, a high-speed train passes. The door rattles, bits of ceiling fall, plaster drops off the wall.)*

REITA. Need a new space.

> (**PINKY** *ignores* **REITA**, *taking a magazine from her bag. As she passes,* **REITA** *strokes* **PINKY**'*s hair.* **PINKY** *recoils.*)

I'll warm up your favourite chilli pasta.

> (*As* **REITA** *heads to the kitchen,* **TANWANT** *rushes out of the cubicle and talks in low, urgent tones to* **PINKY**.)

TANWANT. Ok, gal sun, I no hear from Tej yet – I need to aslap.

PINKY. Chill, you will. (*Looking closely at a pin-up pic.*) Tej is as good as his word as his touch, as his seriously sizzling fit firm hot hot hot body. (*Turns the page.*) Seeing him later, so I'll chase it up yeah? Omg! Look how skinny she is!

TANWANT. (*Looking closely.*) Oof, why she smell of vomit?

> (**PINKY** *snatches away the magazine.* **REITA** *returns with Tupperware and cutlery, scooping food onto two plates.* **TANWANT** *heads back into the cubicle.* **REITA** *holds out a plate for* **PINKY**.)

REITA. Here, one forkful to start with –

PINKY. (*Grabbing the fork and plate.*) I'm not a kid.

> (*Some food falls to the floor, which* **REITA** *cleans up.* **PINKY** *puts down the plate, continues flicking through the magazine.*)

REITA. So, would you like a bigger bedroom?

PINKY. (*Not looking up.*) You moving out?

REITA. We all are.

PINKY. Bagsy your room if you are. But bet you'll give it to one of your two golden boys first.

REITA. Plus ensuite bathroom? Take as long as you want dolling yourself up –

PINKY. Without them banging down the door?

REITA. Ensuite. *(Pause.)* Your own parking space out front?

PINKY. Golden boys will take over that too.

REITA. I'll pay for driving lessons after exams. Buy you a brand new car when you pass.

PINKY. *(Stops flicking through the magazine.)* All this, so I eat your chilli pasta?

REITA. I've found a new house for us all –

PINKY. Ain't moving.

REITA. – and a new Salon space, close by.

PINKY. Good luck.

REITA. In a greener, cleaner town next door.

PINKY. Got my best mates here.

REITA. You can still see them –

PINKY. Yeah, cos I'm not moving.

REITA. Or upgrade to new ones.

PINKY. 'Upgrade?'

REITA. Better schools, more motivated students, higher pass rates –

PINKY. *(Looking up.)* How you paying for it?

REITA. The house –

PINKY. You've already rented out BD – /

REITA. – using our savings – /

PINKY. – and Big Dhadha's old room – /

REITA. – your brothers have well-paid jobs – /

PINKY. – stuck her in the jail box room – /

REITA. – they'll chip in – /

PINKY. – but no way will she ever leave or sell *her* house.

REITA. Have a word in her ear…

PINKY. After drilling through her ear hair and wax? Ewww, DIY.

REITA. I'll buy you a new car, new smartphone –

PINKY. Dad's already getting me a new smartphone – plus anything else I want.

> (**TANWANT** *comes out of the cubicle, to collect some items.*)

REITA. O… K… then eat something…

PINKY. I'm fasting.

REITA. You're what?

PINKY. For Karva Chauth.

REITA. You're not Hindu –

TANWANT. – and no married. You no have husband.

PINKY. For my future husband then. *(To* **TANWANT**.*)* You should do it too.

TANWANT. Fast whole day for future husband? Starve to feed him blessing? Even if I has husband, nahi, no way I starve for him.

REITA. *(To* **PINKY**.*)* Do husbands fast for wives – to return the blessings?

TANWANT. What you think?

PINKY. My future husband will.

REITA. Good luck with that.

TANWANT. *(To* **PINKY.***)* Never know you so religious –

REITA. Even more religious than BD.

PINKY. Yeah, I've even got a tattoo – *(Rolls up her sleeve, then stops.)* Oh shit –

> *(***REITA** *puts down her plate to roll up* **PINKY***'s sleeve.)*

TANWANT. *(Squinting.)* What it is?... An Om?

REITA. Om? Hindu now are you?

PINKY. *(Looking at her tattoo.)* Shit, I asked for an Ek Onkar.

REITA. Has your Dad seen this?

PINKY. Won't care when he does.

REITA. Show BD. Wear a vest, show the gurdwara congregation too.

TANWANT. *(Admiring the tattoo.)* Actually, it look quite nice.

REITA. *(To* **TANWANT.***)* I want your rent, not your opinion.

> *(***TANWANT** *scurries back into the cubicle.)*

If you didn't ask his permission, did you ask mine?

PINKY. Why would I?

REITA. Making up your own rules now?

PINKY. Happens when you grow up.

REITA. Growing up means you can't do what you want all the time.

PINKY. No, it means *you* can't tell me what to do all the time.

REITA. I'm your mother.

PINKY. When you decide?

REITA. Why can't you listen? Like I listened to my Dad?

PINKY. Oh I listen to my Dad. And so what? A friend got a tattoo, paid for mine too.

REITA. Karva Chauth? An Om?

> (**PINKY** *rolls up her other sleeve to reveal a tattoo on her other arm.*)

PINKY. Sikh khanda! Better?

REITA. *(Disbelief.)* Two? You got two tattoos? Cos of a friend?

PINKY. "Councillor Gill's got twelve houses. Boo hoo, I've only got one." One – that isn't even yours!

REITA. *(Rattled.)* It is – mine.

PINKY. I don't compete with my friends. I share with them.

REITA. Cos you're such a devout Sikh with an Om on your arm?

PINKY. And you're such a devout Sikh cos you give fat donations to the gurdwara, even though you never go? Even Dad says so –

REITA. I give when I can. Go when I can.

PINKY. What about praying or doing seva?

REITA. What will you do with your life?

PINKY. Lot more than you're doing with yours.

REITA. Stick with those "friends" telling you an Om is an Ek Onkar –

PINKY. Like our Gurujis said – it's all the same God anyway!

REITA. – and you'll throw your life away!

*(**PINKY** upends the plates and pasta flies everywhere.)*

PINKY. I'm not leaving my friends – or BD's house!

*(**PINKY** storms out of the salon. **TANWANT** rushes out of the cubicle and kneels to pick up the spilled food from the floor.)*

REITA. Thanks Tanni. *(Checking her phone.)* Or I'll be late for the Councillor.

*(**REITA** gathers herself and locks the door, getting herself ready to leave. **TANWANT** cleans up. Loud knocking on the door.)*

Knew she couldn't stay away – *(Opens the salon door, stops abruptly.)* Oh – sorry Kamal, we're at lunch right now.

KAMAL. *(Tearfully.)* Your... your...

REITA. What's wrong?

KAMAL. Your Saas. Told my Saas... –

REITA. Told her what?

KAMAL. – that I was at the station yesterday... that... she – she saw me, from the bridge, by the tracks.

*(**TANWANT** rolls her eyes when she sees **KAMAL**, as **REITA** ushers her into the salon, locking the door after her.)*

My Saas, my husband – they're furious.

REITA. What did BD say?

KAMAL. Girls... like me, come from India, think UK is a life of leisure and luxury. Think our husband's house will be run by servants and machines –

TANWANT. Before you realise you servant *and* machine?

KAMAL. They can't know where I go. That I clean for you. See the trains. But every time your Saas sees me, she tells my Saas –

REITA. *(Dismissively.)* They're just gossiping old bibis –

KAMAL. Gossip for them but –

REITA. *(Cutting her off.)* She won't do it again.

KAMAL. Because sometimes, I have to do things – for me.

REITA. If you don't make time for you, always someone ready to steal it from you.

KAMAL. My Saas likes things done a certain way.

REITA. Like my Saas.

TANWANT. Every Saas.

KAMAL. Perfectly. Just so. If it isn't done her way – do it again – again – again. Do it better. With your eyes shut. So you do it better with your eyes open. Like this, the way I showed you. Do it a hundred times. A thousand. Not like that. Like this. No. This way...

> *(**KAMAL** spots the Reita Faria photo on the desk. Mesmerised, she picks it up. Repeated knocking on the salon door. **BIG DHADHI** stands outside with a blue plastic carrier bag. **TANWANT** moves towards the door but **REITA** pushes her aside to open the door. **BIG DHADHI** tries to move past **REITA**, who strains to keep the conversation in the doorway, to avoid **KAMAL** overhearing.)*

BIG DHADHI. You said he be there.

REITA. *(Dialling on her phone.)* Bloody Harmeet.

BIG DHADHI. Chaddo, he eat by now.

REITA. *(Hanging up.)* No answer. *(Typing a message.)* Why didn't you wait at Giano's?

BIG DHADHI. She no home. I wait on wall. Too cold, walk back.

REITA. He'll be home soon.

BIG DHADHI. Rehnde. I no walk no more. *(Stepping in a little.)*

REITA. *(Blocking* **BIG DHADHI.**) Walking will warm you up –

BIG DHADHI. *(Trying to push into the salon.)* Godhay hurt too much.

REITA. – or get the bus.

BIG DHADHI. Paray ho. I too cold.

> *(As* **REITA** *tries blocking her,* **BIG DHADHI** *slips further through the doorway and sees* **KAMAL,** *who freezes.)*

KAMAL. Sat Sri Akal Auntieji.

BIG DHADHI. Khurio, I just see your Saas – she look for you.

KAMAL. I'm heading home right now.

BIG DHADHI. Say she wait long time. Do all cook, clean, clothe wash today. But you busy here –

REITA. *(To* **BIG DHADHI.**) You need to go –

BIG DHADHI. Where little one?

KAMAL. Nursery.

BIG DHADHI. Your Saas very good with little one. Little one love her lot.

KAMAL. Hanji, she does.

BIG DHADHI. You bless with Saas like that. Look after little one, look after you. Share big house load with you –

KAMAL. Hanji. I've still got housework to do –

BIG DHADHI. Sure your Saas finish it all for you.

> (**KAMAL** *nods.*)

REITA. *(Pushing* **BIG DHADHI** *back out the door.)* Home.

BIG DHADHI. Key.

REITA. He'll be back by the time you get there.

BIG DHADHI. *My* key.

REITA. *(Annoyed.)* Or – just go to the gurdwara –

BIG DHADHI. Give *my* house key.

REITA. Spend the afternoon there, eat langar, pray, gossip about women you don't know –

> (*Pause.* **BIG DHADHI** *leans on the door.*)

BIG DHADHI. Hurt to walk...

REITA. Why did you tell her Saas?

BIG DHADHI. What I say?

REITA. Enough.

BIG DHADHI. All I say her is no good if Saas do everything. Our body carry big bhar, big weight for family. Field there, factory, airport here. Our body break now. No good Saas still carry all thing for all family –

REITA. Before or after you told her Saas she was at the station –?

> (*Pause.*)

BIG DHADHI. *(Tired, holds up the bag.)* Puth, I buy us all kulcha – enough for Tanwant and Kamal –

REITA. We've eaten.

BIG DHADHI. *(Offering the bag, hands shaking.)* Your best kulcha.

REITA. Don't gossip to Kamal's Saas about her.

BIG DHADHI. *(Holding up the bag, hands shaking.)* Amb pickle.

REITA. Save it –

BIG DHADHI. Special –

REITA. – for your son.

BIG DHADHI. – for you... Please my godhay... need to sit.

TANWANT. *(Passing by.)* Aaja BD, I'll napp your knees.

REITA. *(Turns to* **TANWANT.***)* Want to take a long walk too?

> *(***TANWANT** *steps back, concerned.)*

BIG DHADHI. No let me rest here, no let me rest in *my* house –

REITA. Rest at the gurdwara. Gossip with Waheguru as long as you want. He won't mind – he's got eternal time. I've got a busy afternoon, with clients and workers who don't want you gossiping their every move.

BIG DHADHI. *(Folds her hands.)* Mere hath jorhe.

> *(***REITA** *closes and locks the door, moving away. Torn,* **TANWANT** *looks on.* **BIG DHADHI** *touches the glass, then hobbles away.)*

TANWANT. She old womans –

REITA. *(Ignoring* **TANWANT.***)* Kamal, I have to make a quick call.

> *(***KAMAL** *nods, clutching the photo.* **TANWANT** *heads into the cubicle.)*

(Her voice low, on the phone.) Where the hell did you go?... she waited, came back here... she'll head home or to the gurdwara now, so you find her, pick her up... I'm putting in an offer today.

(**REITA** *hangs up. A phone message pings. She reads, collecting her jacket and bag.*)

(*Loudly.*) Tanni, Councillor's waiting – cover for me please.

TANWANT. (*Peering out of the cubicle.*) I no eat lunch yet.

REITA. There's left over pasta.

TANWANT. (*Fed up.*) Haan – and maybe bargain husband will pop out of Tupperware.

(**TANWANT** *heads back into the cubicle.* **KAMAL** *continues staring at the photo.*)

REITA. Sorry about my Saas. It won't happen again. Look, I've got an urgent –

KAMAL. *This* was the photo in your red make-up case.

REITA. (*Stops.*) Yes.

KAMAL. From my wedding day. (*Smiling.*) Miss World.

REITA. Kamal, I've got an urgent –

KAMAL. When I was... at the station... yesterday, I... walked by the train tracks first –

REITA. (*Opening the door.*) I've got to –

KAMAL. I... I saw that woman...

REITA. (*Stops.*) Sangeeta?

KAMAL. I covered Gaggan's eyes. Rushed us out of there.

REITA. Did you try to stop her?

KAMAL. (*Shaking her head.*) I was... too far...

REITA. What were you –?

KAMAL. ...not as brave as... –

(*Pause.*)

before she – … I saw… another woman… older woman… by the tracks…

REITA. Who?

KAMAL. *(Shaking her head.)* It was hazy, in the rain. She was in a white shalwar kameez, chunni flapping in the wind. She was clawing mud. Mud staining the cotton white. She looked up at me. Spoke to me. In whispers.

REITA. What did she say?

KAMAL. She said – she said she was planting lotus seeds –

REITA. Lotus seeds?

KAMAL. – for you.

ACT THREE

Flower

(One week later. Late Afternoon. **REITA** *appears under a spotlight as Miss World Reita Faria, holding a wax cartridge bottle as a microphone.)*

REITA. The judges' scores are in. Final computations have been done. Ladies and Gentleman, it's the big moment! The moment we've all been waiting for! The winner of Miss UK is... Ms. Tanwant Kaur!

> *(***TANWANT*** *steps onto the desk. Flashbulbs pop around her, illuminating her dazzling smile and beauty pageant poses. 'God Save the Queen' plays.* **REITA** *slings a 'MISS UK' sash across* **TANWANT**'*s torso, crowns her with a glittering tiara and presents her with a UK passport, wad of cash and pink lotus that she holds aloft.* **REITA** *disappears into darkness.* **TANWANT** *soaks up the adulation. The spotlight and music fade out as relaxing Indian music fades in.* **REITA** *stares at* **TANWANT** *standing on the desk, waving the cartridge bottle in the air.)*

TANWANT. *(Prodding the ceiling with the bottle.)* I uhm... checking... peeling ceiling...

> *(***REITA*** *sighs, collecting an item from the shelf and is about to return to massaging a*

59

client in a screened cubicle. As she steps down, **TANWANT** *quickly dusts herself down from the crumbling ceiling and hands an envelope to* **REITA**, *which she checks.)*

REITA. Last month and this month?

TANWANT. Every panny.

REITA. I can use this for my two deposits –

TANWANT. Haan, you can pay a lot.

REITA. How did you –?

TANWANT. And – I find husband.

REITA. What?

TANWANT. Marry tomorrow.

REITA. Love marriage then?

TANWANT. Friend...arrange...everything.

REITA. A 'friend'?

TANWANT. No-one you know.

REITA. Someone you know?

TANWANT. Girl do jaldi job.

REITA. Tanni – no trouble...

(**TANWANT** *nods.*)

Listen – Harmeet still hasn't spoken to BD. So I have to. I've stalled the Councillor enough. See her later to make an offer. Once I finish getting the money together, I'll sign, put down a deposit, tomorrow –

TANWANT. Tomorrow?

REITA. So I want nothing – nothing – to mess up my deal with her.

TANWANT. Think I want to get fed, get a bed, in jail? ... Hmmm, no bad idea when I think bout it...

REITA. Or you'll have a husband – but your job.. in the new Salon...

> *(In school uniform,* **PINKY** *bounds in. Frazzled,* **TANWANT** *hurries into the other cubicle.)*

PINKY. Wagwan G?

REITA. I need you to cover for me. I've got to see Councillor Gill.

PINKY. Why?

REITA. A house visit – a... Pampering Package house visit.

PINKY. Cos she's too ballin' posh to come here?

REITA. She's a Councillor.

PINKY. Should visit her ghetto even one time, see how Southall's falling to shit.

REITA. She's a busy lady.

PINKY. Me too. I've got a work experience update at school later –

REITA. I can't miss that appointment.

PINKY. Can't miss mine.

REITA. I'll give you a glowing final report. Tell them you're a natural, ready to run your own salon.

PINKY. *(Starts painting her nails.)* You'll do that anyway. So instead, let me go link with my bae Aisha tonight? For a sleepover study sesh. We've got exams.

REITA. You're asking *me*?

PINKY. Dad already said I can go.

REITA. Cover for me – and only if you promise to study.

PINKY. On Reita Faria's teeny weeny sexy bikini!

REITA. She didn't wear a bikini.

> *(A happy* **PINKY** *pecks a surprised* **REITA** *on the cheek.* **REITA** *heads into the cubicle.* **PINKY** *types on her phone.* **TANWANT** *comes out of the cubicle.)*

TANWANT. Gal sun, I got loan first thing this morning –

PINKY. You did? Mad! Just snapping him now.

TANWANT. Bank process fake document. No question.

PINKY. We in the money honey!

TANWANT. And – he find me husband.

PINKY. Told ya. Tej is just so fast, fit, fine – a peng 'ting!

TANWANT. I get married *(Takes a deep breath.)* – tomorrow!

> *(In hushed tones,* **TANWANT** *and* **PINKY** *gleefully celebrate.)*

PINKY. So you got time to bikini wax me, for my mega mazza night tonight? It's on!

TANWANT. What?

PINKY. It's what Tej wants. What I want. My pay-off.

TANWANT. Then I no marry.

PINKY. Too late. You got a dodgy loan you're not paying back –

TANWANT. Shhhhh!

PINKY. You owe me.

TANWANT. If your Mum know, she rip off my flesh.

PINKY. And you – just rip off my pubes! She won't find out.

TANWANT. Like tattoo?

PINKY. Tanni, most girls do a bikini wax for their boyfriends, don't they?

TANWANT. Get rid of boyfriend then. Do wax for you – when you older. I see grown woman cry, like their inside rip outside. Go red, raw, sore. Hai, hurt me to do it.

PINKY. 'Hai'? It's what you're paid to do.

TANWANT. Finish your GDPE's. So you got choice in life.

PINKY. You'd do it so quick, eyes closed.

TANWANT. Is no right...

PINKY. It's right for Tej and me.

TANWANT. Pinky, no do this. For no man. No run so fast after him, you lose your head, body, to him. No let him take you, from you. After I get pregnant, he run. Haan, he scare. Me also. He leave me all lone. Mummyji drop me. Daddyji drop me. Whole family, village, drop me. Listen me. No do this now. You too young.

PINKY. You just gotta doll me up yeah? For my mega big night.

TANWANT. What bout my meg big day?

PINKY. Oh chill. Tej is gonna handle everything – including me, later!

TANWANT. Ho bas kar. Sharam secret sham wedding, sharam secret wax –

PINKY. UK passport?

*(Exasperated, **TANWANT** paces, then peers through the blinds.)*

TANWANT. Ho ithay aa – what she do out there?

PINKY. *(Peering through the blinds.)* She's tapped, man. Crazy.

TANWANT. Why you think I call her 'Kamali'?

PINKY. Crazy. Like she's going somewhere –

TANWANT. – then walk straight back where she come from.

PINKY. Swear Mums she's always at the station. On the platform, I get shook when fast trains speed past. Think someone will chuck a brick from a window, so I always turn my back, so they mash up my head, not my face. But that Freshie freak yeah – just stands there – and watches – the trains. Just stands there…and watches. Crosses the yellow line, pushes her daughter's pram so close to the edge –

TANWANT. Haan, sometime I see her with pram – but no daughter. Push empty pram one end of road to other, then back, then back again.

PINKY. Like one of those spirits drifting by the tracks.

> (**TANWANT** *snaps the blinds shut, turns and freezes.*)

TANWANT. Haah, she catch my eye!

PINKY. Shit, she's heading in!

> (**PINKY** *slides across the floor and takes selfies on her phone.* **TANWANT** *rushes to the desk.* **KAMAL** *walks in.*)

KAMAL. I need to speak to her.

TANWANT. *(Pointing to the cubicle.)* Client.

KAMAL. Please.

TANWANT. No disturb.

KAMAL. I'll be quick.

TANWANT. *(Sighing.)* She say no, you come later.

    (**KAMAL** *nods.* **TANWANT** *knocks on the cubicle.*)

(*To* **REITA**.) Kamali here to see you.

    (**REITA** *comes out, wiping her hands.* **TANWANT** *raises her eyebrows at* **PINKY**.)

KAMAL. Reita, sorry to disturb but can I collect my wage, now?

REITA. Sure.

    (**REITA** *takes money out of* **TANWANT**'*s rent envelope in her handbag, as* **TANWANT** *looks on in disbelief.* **REITA** *hands* **KAMAL** *the cash.*)

KAMAL. Thank you.

REITA. . Still OK for cleaning the salon later?

KAMAL. Hanji. Thank you again.

    (**KAMAL** *rushes out of the Salon.* **REITA** *heads back into the cubicle.* **TANWANT** *and* **PINKY** *look at each other, bemused, shaking their heads.*)

PINKY. Last week, her first time 'cleaning' the house, I was Facetiming Tej, watching 'Jebo' –

TANWANT. 'Jebo'! Sachi good drama! When it come on, I bang patila on shed wall for shut up alley addicts. Poor Jebo, push round by husband, sis-in-law, Saas –

PINKY. ...and that Kamali yeah, tries hoovering between my perfectly painted, manicured toes. Like I've got dirt stuck between them. Should hoover her own Freshie toes. Bet they're filthy.

TANWANT. She pher hoover like she beating lathi stick, rub cloth half hour same spot like she rub out her brains –

PINKY. Then, she knocked a bucket of water all over the floor. Dad helped clean it up. I wasn't going to. And get this – in Mum and Dad's room, I saw her at the dressing table, about to try on Mum's jewellery.

TANWANT. Nahi...

PINKY. Told her to put it down.

TANWANT. No sharam.

PINKY. She pretended she was just cleaning, carried on like nothing happened.

TANWANT. Reita say, 'No wage rise, where your rent?' But give her wage isn't it?

PINKY. If you call a few quid a week a wage.

TANWANT. Best you not know how much your Mum pay me then.

PINKY. People gotta be paid their worth. That's why Tej slays it.

TANWANT. Why Reita give her job in Salon *and* house? She know her one week –

PINKY. Care in the community? Charity? Who knows? She's a wasteman. Anyway, keeps Mum off my case bout the cleaning.

>   *(In her anorak,* **BIG DHADHI** *hobbles into the Salon.* **TANWANT** *embraces her.)*

TANWANT. Sat Sri Akal BD! You no come ek whole week. We miss you!

BIG DHADHI. Big boss here?

>   *(***TANWANT** *points to the cubicle.)*

PINKY. *(Tugs* **BIG DHADHI***'s beard.)* BD, Mum wants me to be a beautician like her –

BIG DHADHI. No be your Mum. Be you.

PINKY. *(Tugs* **BIG DHADHI***'s beard.)* Aaja, I'll chop it off –

> *(***BIG DHADHI*** slaps* **PINKY***'s hand. She sits on a chair, pressing her knees.)*

BIG DHADHI. Why, when man grow big beard, people call it wisdom? When woman grow big beard, they make big joke?

> *(***PINKY*** picks up an electrolysis pen and waves it at* **BIG DHADHI***.)*

PINKY. Mum's got all this new dope laser stuff. If we zap your beard, it won't ever grow back.

BIG DHADHI. I take amrit.

PINKY. So what if you're baptised? The Ten Gurujis will understand.

TANWANT. BD, Sikh people has to live with overgrow hair back then. With electrolysis and IPL, you no has to.

BIG DHADHI. Bad womans take out hair, take out root. Pinky, you watch TV all time. Hair like TV aerial to Waheguru. We peoples, we lost, need hair for fine-tune to Waheguru. If peoples rip out hair, how we get reception to Waheguru?

PINKY. *(Waving the pen at* **BIG DHADHI***.)* You had an accident –

TANWANT. Big roti accident!

PINKY. You were making rotis for Dad and the boys and the kitchen towel caught fire on the thava, burnt your beard clean off!

BIG DHADHI. Ho bakwaas na kar.

TANWANT. BD, you always make the roti at home?

BIG DHADHI. You think Reita make?

TANWANT. She say she do.

BIG DHADHI. If she make, her nylon nail fall in Harmeet roti. He fed up eating nail polish roti. And he say, 'After 25 year, her roti still look like wiggly maps of Punjab'.

(**PINKY** *and* **TANWANT** *laugh loudly, quickly stifling their laughs.*)

Like how she tell everyone she 45. But really she 50?

PINKY. She lies bout her age?

BIG DHADHI. Tanni know – in India, in old time, we not know what is birthday.

TANWANT. I no even know my real age.

PINKY. See – you were born to fake it to make it!

BIG DHADHI. When boy like your Daddyji born, we make Hindu star chart. No for girl like Reita. So when we people first come UK, we member boy birth date. Never girl birth date. We make up birthday for all girl passport. Reita Daddyji no member her real age. So he make her passport age five year young. Her Mummyji member Reita real age later. But Reita keep passport age. She change age like she change name. Mummyji spell it R.I.T.A. when she born. Reita change it later, cos she think she Miss World.

> (**PINKY** *and* **TANWANT** *laugh loudly.* **REITA** *comes out.*)

REITA. Keep it down! (*Sees* **BIG DHADHI**.) Good – you're here.

BIG DHADHI. Pinky, napp my knees. Aaja.

REITA. I'm almost done, then Tanni, clean up after me.

> (**TANWANT** *nods.* **REITA** *heads back into the cubicle.*)

BIG DHADHI. (*Points to head.*) Up here, I walk so fast. But chhil shell body no walk so fast...

(PINKY presses BIG DHADHI's knees. TANWANT types away on her phone.)

PINKY. BD, some girls like taking off hair from down there.

BIG DHADHI. Kitho? *(Looks down.)* Leg? Toe? I got very long toe hair – *(Touches PINKY's hair.)* long as your head hair.

PINKY. No, down there!

BIG DHADHI. *(Looks all over the floor.)* Down where?

PINKY. *(Giggles and points below.)* They take off hair from their –

BIG DHADHI. *(Still looking around the floor.)* Where?

PINKY. Phudis!

(TANWANT covers her mouth in horror. PINKY bursts into laughter.)

BIG DHADHI. Dur fitteh mooh!

(BIG DHADHI covers her face with her chunni. TANWANT and PINKY stifle laughter.)

(Confused.) Why?

TANWANT. No nasty tangle.

BIG DHADHI. Ho Rabba, how much dark fall when woman be girl?

PINKY. How much dark fall when old woman be old man?

BIG DHADHI. Girl no be girl? Woman no be woman?

PINKY. Bearded woman be bearded woman and bearded man be bearded man?

BIG DHADHI. Sachi! Girl try be old. Woman try be young. Ek run forward too fast. Ek run back too fast. Crash! Who happy?

PINKY. If I had –

(**REITA** *comes out, with her red make-up case, gesturing to keep the noise down.*)

– a bikini wax done –

REITA. You won't.

PINKY. *(Ignores* **REITA***.)* I'd have a thin line of hair running from my stomach to *(Points below.)* down there –

REITA. We don't do bikini waxes on young girls –

PINKY. Says the beauty pimp. *(To* **TANWANT***.)* What do they call that line?

TANWANT. Landing strip.

BIG DHADHI. Like at airport?

PINKY. *(Enacts an aeroplane motion with her hands.)* When the landing strip has been laid, the airplane comes flying into laaaaand!

(**PINKY** *laughs hysterically.* **TANWANT** *shakes her head.* **BIG DHADHI** *is silent.* **REITA** *hushes* **PINKY***, brings out a client and waves her off.*)

REITA. *(Points to the other cubicle.)* Tanni, clean up now please. Pinky, shadow Tanni, learn something.

PINKY. *(Still giggling, holding her phone.)* Or I could just snapchat with –

REITA. Revision session?

PINKY. I'll shadow.

(**TANWANT** *heads into the cubicle with* **PINKY**. **REITA** *puts away the client's cash payment.*)

BIG DHADHI. Nahi, you no pluck my beard now we lone –

REITA. Did Harmeet talk to you?

BIG DHADHI. He say you talk to me.

REITA. Course he did.

BIG DHADHI. No let him do anything, then haan, he do nothing.

REITA. Where did he learn that?

BIG DHADHI. What you want?

REITA. BD, it's time to move out, move up, move on.

BIG DHADHI. *(Getting up.)* Theek ya but I just get here.

REITA. We've found a new house. A bigger one.

BIG DHADHI. *(Sitting down.)* 'We'?

REITA. You'll have a bigger bedroom –

BIG DHADHI. *(Pointing to the cubicle.)* Big, like that room?

REITA. We'll all have much more space –

BIG DHADHI. That you no let me use in day?

REITA. A big, expensive house other people wish they lived in. I'll open a new Salon close by –

BIG DHADHI. Close to gurdwara?

REITA. You can still get a bus – or two – there.

BIG DHADHI. Haan, easy for me.

REITA. Pinky needs to be away from here.

BIG DHADHI. Always run, paj paj.

REITA. Better for us all.

BIG DHADHI. Tanwant?

REITA. What about her?

(**BIG DHADHI** *shakes her head.*)

Big Dhada and you have given us so much already –

BIG DHADHI. Haan, for you.

REITA. Now, it's our turn to build something for the boys and Pinky.

BIG DHADHI. Haan, for them.

REITA. Time to move – to this *(Shows photos on her phone.)*. Beautiful hunnah? Proper English kothi.

BIG DHADHI. What you want?

REITA. The house. The boys and us will put in the rest of the money.

BIG DHADHI. My house – my saving too?

> *(**REITA** takes out papers from the case and presents them to **BIG DHADHI**.)*

REITA. *(Points.)* Just sign here and…here.

> *(**REITA** gives **BIG DHADHI** a pen. **BIG DHADHI** pretends to read.)*

You can't read English.

BIG DHADHI. I understand.

REITA. I can explain it all to you.

BIG DHADHI. Where I sign?

REITA. *(Points.)* Right here.

> *(**BIG DHADHI** holds the pen. She puts the pen to the page and holds it there. Pause. Her hand shakes. She stops.)*

BIG DHADHI. I always think I die in that house, like Harmeet Dad. His last breath, I hold him there.

> *(**REITA** checks the time on her phone.)*

REITA. I know – but BD, I really need –

BIG DHADHI. He still talk me there, when no-one else do.

> *(**REITA**'s phone pings. She reads the message.)*

When people laugh me, he khich my beard, make me laugh. *(Laughs.)*

> *(Distracted,* **REITA** *falls in with the laughter, while typing a message on her phone.)*

I see him, hear him, feel him so close there –

REITA. *(Distracted by her phone.)* I know you miss him BD. So we'll put a big TV in your new room to watch your Punjabi channels from bed, like I do.

BIG DHADHI. Only once, he no with me, when I need him. When I first come UK, Gora man –

REITA. *(Distracted by her phone.)* You'll love the huge garden. You can have your own small patch to grow plants, vegetables, like when you first came here –

BIG DHADHI. Every day, thirty year, I work same Heathrow, same Terminal 3. To buy house. Every day, I scrub, clean, scrub, clean. But I never wipe it way, Every night, I run to Harmeet Dad. He never leave me gain. He still in house with me.

REITA. *(Putting her phone away, points.)* Just sign here.

> *(***BIG DHADHI** *puts pen to paper again. Pause. Her hand shakes. She hurls the pen and papers.)*

BIG DHADHI. Nahi, you no steal my house!

REITA. BD, I'm not –

BIG DHADHI. You lone, with nothing, when I marry you with Harmeet. No house! No Salon! I take you in when peoples gossip bout your Mummyji, Daddyji – you. I run house, make roti, wash, paal your kids, so you work. Why I no open my door when wish? Close when wish? You take my key. Now you take *my* house?

> *(***REITA** *picks up the pen and papers and thrusts the pen back at* **BIG DHADHI**.*)*

REITA. For our family.

BIG DHADHI. Leave my house lone.

REITA. All our futures, the children's futures –

BIG DHADHI. Your future.

> (**REITA** *tries to force* **BIG DHADHI** *to take the pen.*)

REITA. Please. Sign.

> (**BIG DHADHI** *pushes away the pen and* **REITA,** *who takes a breath.*)

Will you just sign?

BIG DHADHI. I die lone in *my* house. Die lone in *my* town.

> (*Pause.*)

REITA. I'll make sure you die all alone in an old people's home – in a town, far from here.

BIG DHADHI. Haan, push me out like you push out your Mummyji?

> (**REITA** *stops. She grabs the papers, collects her things and storms out of the salon.* **BIG DHADHI** *slumps on a chair.*)

(*Calling aloud.*) Pinky? Pinky? I tired. I want go home. Home…

> (**BIG DHADHI** *covers her face with her chunni and falls asleep. Through a silhouetted cubicle screen,* **PINKY** *takes off her clothes down to her underwear. She climbs onto the beauty couch, while* **TANWANT** *snaps on latex gloves. With* **PINKY** *in various positions,* **TANWANT** *smoothes on hot wax and removes strips of hair from* **PINKY**'s *bikini area. The stripping sounds continue loudly for a while,*

eventually fading as lights dim in the cubicle.
The Salon darkens. A door sounds. **PINKY** *and*
TANWANT *slip out in the darkness. A street*
lamp illuminates sleeping **BIG DHADHI**. *The*
desk phone rings. **BIG DHADHI** *wakes, listens,*
until the phone stops ringing. She sits up,
restless and disorientated, flicking her mala
beads.)

Member when I first arrive? You ready here – here
seven year. I step off cloud. Step off plane. Stand in
line. Wait. But you no there. Gora man in uniform pull
me out. Ehni dhar. I so scare. So scare. Where he take
me? Lock me in chitta white room. Jadi thand. Too
cold. Where I am? Jail? UK? Or worse, Pakistan? I sit.
All lone. Stare at door. Wait. Hold bag tight you buy
me from bazaar, when you marry me. Press mala beads
in my hand, one your Mummyji give when you marry
me. Where you is? No here. *(Pause.)* Gora doctor come.
Give paper. Say me 'sign'. I shake. No understand. He
put my hand on pen, pen on paper. My hand shake. If
I sign, he send me back? Way from you? If I no sign,
he send me back? Way from you? I sign. No write my
name. Write my God. Ek Onkar. *(Pause.)* He point
my clothes. Kaprey lah. *(Flaps at her anorak.)* I take
off coat. He say 'gain. Take off kaprey. He do action.
Chakkar. Head spin. Heart beat so fast. Breath so fast.
Breath so loud. He more loud. He say 'gain – take off
kaprey.

> *(Pause.* **BIG DHADHI** *shakes, cries, unravelling*
> *her hair, taking off her clothes, down to her*
> *white vest, kacchera shorts and a small Sikh*
> *kirpan, slung across her torso.)*

I peel my kaprey – like I peel my skin. *(Pause.)* Only
you see me nangi, no clothe. Only you touch me. Why
he see me nangi? See my body? Why he touch me?
Down there? *(Pause.)* You my husband. Where you is?

(Pause.) I look for you 'gain. You no here. I wait you. Where you is?

I cover with kameez. Doctor take my kameez. Push me on bed. Put rubber glove. Shink davai. From bottle to cotton. Pull my leg open. Push cotton. Wipe. Take out. I so scare. So scare.

He open my leg, see if I pure. If pure, I stay UK. No pure, I go back. He say me I no pure. I say I marry Harmeet Dad in India, before Harmeet Dad come UK. I come UK join him. But he say no pure, go back. I say him no. I got all paper. He say go back.

But I no move. No move. Say I has right. They check 'gain. See I has right paper, visa and haan, I marry to you. I has right to be here. I has right! Be here with husband, who work UK factory, day, night. I no lie. Those gora mans know they wrong. But no say sorry. No ever say sorry. How UK, with womans Prime Minister, Rani Queen, how UK do this to womans like us?

> *(**BIG DHADHI** hears a noise and stares at the shadow of a woman moving across the salon door outside and then stares at a moving silhouette on the cubicle screen, inside.)*

Who it is? … You?

> *(A 1960s Hindi film song, of longing, love and loss, streams out of the cubicle. In her vest and kacchera, **BIG DHADHI** glimpses **KAMAL**, in a shalwar kameez, her hair unpinned, trying on lipsticks and nail varnishes, twirling out under her red wedding dupatta. **KAMAL** cries as she sings and slowly dances.)*

Doctor? Is you? Doctor?

> *(**KAMAL** gasps. She quickly turns off the music on her phone, wipes her tears and*

make up, gathers her hair and straightens
her dupatta.)

KAMAL. Auntieji, it's… it's… Kamal.

BIG DHADHI. Doctor, why you play Harmeet Dad best song?

KAMAL. Theek ya?

BIG DHADHI. I got right be here. Main tuhanu dassdi, I got right!

KAMAL. *(Holds* **BIG DHADHI.***)* Auntieji, it's me – Kamal.

BIG DHADHI. *(Looks at herself.)* I peel off kaprey, like I peel off skin.

KAMAL. Why?

BIG DHADHI. *(Whispering, pointing to the other cubicle.)* Doctor, he took off my kaprey –

*(*KAMAL *checks the other cubicle.)*

KAMAL. Auntieji, there's no-one in there.

BIG DHADHI. But… he – he –

*(*KAMAL *collects* **BIG DHADHI***'s clothes.)*

KAMAL. Here, let me put these on you.

*(*KAMAL *helps* **BIG DHADHI** *put on her clothes.*
Pause.)

BIG DHADHI. Where Reita? What you do her?

KAMAL. She gave me the key, to clean the Salon.

BIG DHADHI. I got key too. *(Pulls out an old key from her kameez pocket.)* From Harmeet Dad suitcase. China lodger girl take down. *(Gives the key to* **KAMAL.***)* Reita no take.

KAMAL. Keep it safe.

(**KAMAL** *gives the key back to* **BIG DHADHI,**
who carefully puts it in her pocket.)

BIG DHADHI. I no let her take.

KAMAL. Not if it opens a door for you.

BIG DHADHI. (*Putting the key away.*) You right khurio.
You right. (*Rubs her back.*) Hai, sleep on beauty chair,
like sleep on bed of nails.

KAMAL. (*Smiles.*) You didn't sleep well?

BIG DHADHI. Dream of Harmeet Dad. He stand other side
of river. Buffalo, cart, tractor, pass in middle, on water.
He smile me. Say nothing.

KAMAL. (*Smiling.*) Keeping an eye on you...

BIG DHADHI. With his big NHS glasses. I hold out my
hand. He smile gain. Walk away.

KAMAL. Knows you're strong without him...

(**KAMAL** *kneels in front of* **BIG DHADHI,**
slipping on her shoes. **BIG DHADHI** *notices
a mark on* **KAMAL**'*s neck. Teary-eyed, she
touches it.*)

BIG DHADHI. Puth... I no make trouble –

KAMAL. (*Holding* **BIG DHADHI**'*s hand, weepy.*) I know...

BIG DHADHI. When I see you at station...

KAMAL. I like to go there.

(**BIG DHADHI** *nods.*)

I like reaching out my hand, touching the train,
running with it.

(**BIG DHADHI** *holds* **KAMAL** *close to her.*)

(*Gathering herself.*) Aaja, I'll take you home.

BIG DHADHI. Nahi, you be late. Saas be angry.

KAMAL. I won't let you go alone.

BIG DHADHI. Puth, what they do?

> (**KAMAL** *is silent. She bows her head.* **BIG DHADHI** *touches her head, blessing* **KAMAL.**)

ACT FOUR

Bloom

(Late afternoon. The 'Open/Closed' sign is set to 'Closed'. Low-level Punjabi romantic songs and bhangra music play in the salon. Coconuts, garlands, kalire and a 'CONGRATULATIONS' banner decorate the interior. **REITA** *applies make-up to* **TANWANT**, *who wears a red and gold wedding blouse and lengha, with red and white choora bangles on her wrists.* **REITA** *dabs red and white bindi dots above* **TANWANT**'s *eyebrows.* **TANWANT** *shakes her bangled hands to dry her mehndi. The salon door rattles.* **REITA** *lets in* **PINKY**, *in school uniform. She takes off her coat, hurls her bag aside.)*

REITA. *(To* **PINKY**.*)* Hurry, so we can finish Tanni.

PINKY. *(Looking around, to* **REITA**.*)* You did this?

TANWANT. Me. My big day nahi? Even coconuts! Good luck gift from me to me.

REITA. *(Hands* **PINKY** *nail varnish.)* Top-coat on Tanni's nails.

PINKY. *(Admiring* **TANWANT**.*)* Wow, check out Miss Punjab, soon to be Mrs. UK!

TANWANT. Haan, how lucky he is.

PINKY. *(Painting* **TANWANT***'s nails.)* So where you get the lengha?

TANWANT. Your Mum hire last-minute gift. *(To* **REITA***.)* Come on, where you get –?

REITA. Top secret.

TANWANT. *(Looks at* **PINKY** *in horror.)* Oh no!

PINKY. Not Miss World's – but Miss Weirdo's?

REITA. *(To* **TANWANT***.)* Kamal's roughly the same size.

TANWANT. *(Pinching the lengha all over.)* Hai, hai, hai, hai, hai!

PINKY. *(Moving away.)* Bet the armpits stink! Cleavage area and crotch –!

TANWANT. *(Turning her head away.)* I dare no smell it!

REITA. She dry-cleaned it first.

TANWANT. Ho Rabba! Kamali lengha, fake husband, fake guest, fake photographer, registry office – how Miss Punjab village catch marry like this?

PINKY. I'm gonna get married in a designer lengha yeah, seven star hotel, hundreds of guests, wicked DJ, flashin' dancefloor, big screens all round, devoted only to me –

REITA. Who'll pay for all that?

PINKY. Bride's family always do. So you. *(To* **TANWANT***.)* Your hands are shaking. Stop it.

TANWANT. *(Looking at her hands.)* Your Mum did mehndi so pretty isn't it?

PINKY. That's waaay too light...

TANWANT. Vadiya. Peoples say, 'Darker mehndi, stronger husband's love'.

PINKY. Lately, mine's been so dark yeah.

TANWANT. Hai, mine so light, even mehndi know this fake marriage.

REITA. *(To* **TANWANT.***)* Be glad you're not marrying for real. Rather than becoming inseparable in old age with the man you marry – you pull apart –

TANWANT. *This* Bridal Package? No sure I want this bit –

REITA. Youth is an open road. When you're older, only cul-de-sacs.

PINKY. What's a 'cul-de-sex'?

TANWANT. Like street where Sangeeta murder?

REITA. 'Sac'! A dead-end road.

TANWANT. *(To* **REITA.***)* You really know how to get womans in mood for marriage. No wonder Bridal Package top-seller.

> *(The salon door rattles.* **PINKY** *opens the door to* **BIG DHADHI***, embracing her. Under her anorak,* **BIG DHADHI** *wears a white chunni and shalwar kameez.)*

PINKY. BD, so sorry we forgot you here yesterday.

TANWANT. Haan BD, I was worried about wedding, Pinky had to – study –

> *(***BIG DHADHI** *shakes her head, waves her hand dismissively.)*

BIG DHADHI. *(Giving a thumbs up to* **TANWANT.***)* You look like real voti bride.

TANWANT. You look like you dressed for funeral.

BIG DHADHI. Sangeeta.

REITA. *(Stops, to* **TANWANT.***)* Today?

TANWANT. Ho Rabba, how we forget?

PINKY. *(To* **BIG DHADHI.***)* You'll meet her husband!

REITA. *(To* **TANWANT.***)* We should have gone.

BIG DHADHI. *(Sitting.)* Still time...

REITA. *(To* **TANWANT.***)* I've got an important meeting soon –

> *(A knock on the Salon door.)*

TANWANT. *(Peering.)* Ho dekho – Miss Weirdo here! Living crazy name.

PINKY. Needs a restraining order slapped on her.

REITA. *(To* **PINKY.***)* Let her in.

TANWANT. I only marry later but Kamali make everyone more Kamali every time she turn up.

> *(***PINKY*** reluctantly opens the door, keeping* **KAMAL** *at the door with a fake smile.)*

KAMAL. I came to see –

PINKY. We're busy –

REITA. Pinky.

KAMAL. *(Sees* **BIG DHADHI.***)* Sat Sri Akal Auntieji.

BIG DHADHI. Kidda puth? Aaja –

> *(Annoyed,* **PINKY** *reluctantly steps aside.)*

REITA. Hi Kamal.

> *(***KAMAL*** enters, holding a dripping lotus, unsettling* **REITA. TANWANT** *and* **PINKY** *exchange glances.* **KAMAL** *touches* **BIG DHADHI***'s feet, then sees* **TANWANT** *in her lengha and stares.)*

BIG DHADHI. Puth... Theek ya? ...

KAMAL. *(Forcing a smile.)* Hanji Auntieji... Thusi?

BIG DHADHI. *(Smiling.)* Life chaldi.

KAMAL. *(To* **TANWANT.***)* … Fits…perfectly…

TANWANT. Too big, specially round stomach – and chest.

KAMAL. I couldn't breathe in it.

PINKY. *(To* **KAMAL.***)* Hope you washed it since.

> (**KAMAL** *begins to hold out the dripping lotus for* **REITA.***)*

REITA. How kind to bring Tanwant a flower on her wedding day.

> (**KAMAL** *awkwardly adjusts and holds out the lotus for* **TANWANT,** *who exchanges bemused glances with* **PINKY.***)*

KAMAL. *(To* **TANWANT.***)* For – you.

TANWANT. *(Takes the lotus.)* For what?

KAMAL. Good luck.

TANWANT. Thanks Kamali but –

PINKY. Ewww, loads of mud on it –

TANWANT. Where you find it?

KAMAL. By the train tracks –

PINKY. Where the crackheads hang out?

TANWANT. So many khat-smoking Somali there –

PINKY. Drunken Polish too –

TANWANT. People from outside, coming in, taking over –

KAMAL. The lotus was all alone, blooming, above muddy water. I couldn't leave it there, with the plastic bags, beer cans –

PINKY. – crack pipes, smack needles –

BIG DHADHI. Pinky –

KAMAL. – so I reached in. Root came out clean, stalk so
long.

REITA. You were at the station?

> (**PINKY** *and* **TANWANT** *make faces at each
> other.*)

KAMAL. (*Strokes the air.*) Trains speeding so fast, slicing
the numbness –

> (**REITA** *takes a deep breath.*)

REITA. (*To* **PINKY**, *pointing at the lotus.*) Put it in water –

KAMAL. – cold rush washing over me.

REITA. (*To* **PINKY**.) – in the back, please.

PINKY. (*Holding up her nail varnish.*) I'm busy.

REITA. (*To* **PINKY**.) Will you –?

PINKY. Time's ticking for Tanni.

> (*As* **KAMAL** *watches, agitated* **REITA** *takes the
> lotus, carrying it into the back.*)

BIG DHADHI. (*To* **KAMAL**.) Puth, lotus die quick out of
water. Should left it there.

KAMAL. Auntieji, I couldn't.

BIG DHADHI. Lotus grow in mud. But lotus beauty so
strong, bloom above it.

KAMAL. Muddier the water, more beautiful the lotus when
it blooms.

> (**KAMAL** *rests her head against the salon door,
> looking back at* **TANWANT** *and* **PINKY**, *who
> are taking silly wedding selfies.*)

BIG DHADHI. Used to be so many lotus in Punjab –

KAMAL. Mummyji called me Kamal after them. So few left there now...

BIG DHADHI. When I little girl, I used to roll shalwar over godhay – strong godhay. Step in dirty water. Shoo way bee. Grab lotus. Pop lotus seed, like popcorn, Pinky. Sleep sachi sweet sleep. But Naniji always warn me – eat too much lotus, you fall deep sleep, forget who you is, where you come from.

> (**REITA** *returns empty-handed and continues applying* **TANWANT**'s *make up.*)

(*Glancing at* **REITA**.) When I come UK, I see many people – think 'They eat this lotus?' Cos they sleep sachi deep sleep in money, make-up, me-me-me dream... forget who they is, where they from.

PINKY. The lotus also make you paagal, mad innit? That's why it's called Kamal?

BIG DHADHI. Pinky, chup kar, help me up.

> (**PINKY** *helps up* **BIG DHADHI**. **BIG DHADHI** *holds out a cash note for* **TANWANT**.)

Puth, small wedding pyaar.

TANWANT. (*Refusing.*) Nahi, nahi BD, I no take. Nahi –

BIG DHADHI. (*Pushing the note into* **TANWANT**'s *hand.*) Khurio, I no fight no more. Take, marry, get UK passport.

> (**REITA** *shakes her head.* **TANWANT** *and* **PINKY**'s *faces drop.*)

KAMAL. 'Passport?'

TANWANT/PINKY. BD!

BIG DHADHI. (*To* **TANWANT**.) Sorry puth.

KAMAL. I promise I won't say anything.

TANWANT. Or I tell your Saas few thing.

BIG DHADHI. *(To* **TANWANT.***)* Kamal bahuth good girl –
she no say nothing no-one.

REITA. *(To* **BIG DHADHI.***)* Nor you.

BIG DHADHI. *(To* **TANWANT**, *zips her mouth shut.)* Mooh
bhand.

> *(***BIG DHADHI** *circles* **TANWANT***'s head with
> the note, places it in her lap. She blesses*
> **KAMAL**, *touching her head, as* **PINKY** *helps*
> **BIG DHADHI** *out the door.)*

KAMAL. I wish I had a passport wedding.

TANWANT. Nahi Kamali, you no wish. You has husband,
daughter, job – UK dream –

KAMAL. After dropping off Auntieji yesterday, I got back
late. He was out til much later. My Saas told him this
morning. Then, they did what they always do…

REITA. What?

> *(***KAMAL** *hesitates.)*

What did they do?

KAMAL. Shout. Spit. Slap. Punch. Push me to the floor.
Into walls. Doors. Pound my flesh. My head. Tear my
clothes, my hair…

> *(Silence.)*

PINKY.	**TANWANT.**
Shit./	Hai Rabba –

REITA. Kamal –

KAMAL. I used to grow flowers, plants in the back garden.
Marigolds, tomatoes, chillies… Like home. *(Pause.)*
When my boy was stillborn, they cemented the back
garden. When my girl was born, they cemented over

my flowers, plants in the front. Now I just squat on the ground, tearing out weeds from cracks in the cement.

(Pause.)

I know Gaggan hears. But she doesn't cry –

REITA. Won't sleep til he does?

KAMAL. They say I'm mad.

REITA. They can't beat you like that.

KAMAL. I was never modern enough. British enough. Beautiful enough. Always something wrong. Something he wants to beat out of me... Why marry when they can't be husbands, fathers, sons? ... Yet to feel beautiful, cover our own marks and scars, we women tell them they're men. Never face the ugly lies we tell ourselves. Tell each other.

> *(**REITA** reaches out to **KAMAL**, brushing **KAMAL**'s face and hair. Pause.)*

*(To **REITA**.)* When I picked the lotus today, I saw her again.

> *(**REITA** nods, teary-eyed. **PINKY** and **TANWANT** exchange perplexed glances.)*

Did he make her feel like she was the ugliest woman in the world?

REITA. *(Wiping tears.)* He wasn't the only one.

KAMAL. *(To **REITA**.)* They called her crazy too, didn't they?

REITA. They weren't the only ones.

KAMAL. How crazy was she?

> *(**REITA** is silent, trying to hold back tears. Pause.)*

After I saw her, I found this, buried by the tracks.

(**KAMAL** *takes a hastily wrapped object from her jacket pocket and holds it out for* **REITA.** **REITA** *opens it. She lifts out an ornate bottle of surma and gasps.*)

TANWANT. A bottle of surma?

REITA. My Mum had one...exactly...like this.

KAMAL. *(Backing out.)* I've got to go –

TANWANT. *(To* **KAMAL.***)* Don't put up with it.

KAMAL. – pick up my daughter –

PINKY. Leave them.

TANWANT. Places you can go, people who help.

REITA. *(To* **KAMAL.***)* If you need anything – anything –

KAMAL. *(To* **TANWANT.***)* I hope the lengha brings you more joy than me.

TANWANT. I hope so too. Or I get criminal record, not UK passport. Kamal, I return lengha when –

(**KAMAL** *rushes out.*)

She be ok?

REITA. *(Turning the bottle over in her hand, to* **TANWANT.***)* You're getting late.

PINKY. She really find that there, Mum?

REITA. *(Turning the bottle.)* My Mum would sit me on the bed. Paint my lips. My cheeks. Bring out colour where blood had drained. A gold bottle like this on the dresser. She'd take out the dipping stick. Lift my eyelid. Gently hold it open. Cold metal pressing the edge. Black surma running against pink flesh. Line my eyes. She said – the way men lined their eyes before battle. Streak my eyes pink to black.

TANWANT. Cos you think she try to make you beautiful. Really she try to kill you with lead poison –

REITA. Beauty hurts doesn't it?

TANWANT. Nahi, beauty kill. But one day not gonna hurt is it? Specially in passport marriage! Reita, where our surma? Streak pink to black like your Mummyji did!

> (**REITA** *feels the bottle in her hand and puts it down.*)

Come on, for your Mummyji!

> (**REITA** *takes a fresh bottle of surma from the shelf and applies it to* **TANWANT**'*s eyes. She hooks a tikka through* **TANWANT**'*s hair and fixes a bright red bindi on her forehead.* **PINKY** *takes out a fake gold haar necklace from its case and drapes it around* **TANWANT**'*s neck.*)

PINKY. In the name of Ash and Sush, I declare you Miss UK!

REITA. (*To* **TANWANT**.) You're good to go.

TANWANT. I not a snack Reita. I the blushing bride.

> (**TANWANT** *stares in the mirror. She takes exaggerated deep breaths.* **PINKY** *takes photos of a posing* **TANWANT** *on her phone.*)

PINKY. British husband, UK passport, it's what you want –

> (*A car outside sounds its horn.* **TANWANT** *peers through the door.*)

TANWANT. (*Hyper-ventilating.*) O-ho, he's here!

PINKY. (*Peering though the door.*) A Freshie's driving you there?

REITA. He's got a driving licence?

TANWANT. No passport and visa too. But then I never met husband, so...

> (**TANWANT** *collects her clutch purse. She opens the door and waves at the driver, before stepping back inside and closing the door.*)

(Panicking.) How many passport wedding go wrong?

REITA. Do not mention the Salon –

PINKY. Chill, you're in experienced hands.

REITA. *(To* **PINKY.***)* Is she?

PINKY. They must have done it so many times before.

TANWANT. Paj from Punjab...paj here...maybe better keep running, no do this...

REITA. Face it.

TANWANT. *(Calming down, to* **REITA.***)* Oil and water?

PINKY. For Freshie car?

TANWANT. Mummyji would insist.

REITA. *(Rushing to the backroom.)* I'll get them.

> (**TANWANT** *opens the door and signals to the driver she will be out soon.*)

PINKY. Oil and water?

TANWANT. You bless me with hand of innocence and purity –

PINKY. Yeah about that. See, last night –

TANWANT. *(Holds up her hand.)* Nahi –

PINKY. Tej and me –

TANWANT. Youngest daughter always give blessing –

PINKY. We did –

TANWANT. – and she get paid to do it –

PINKY. How much innocence you want?

TANWANT. We drip oil both side, door outside. You hold glass water out there. When I step over door, I drop shiny one pound coin in water –

PINKY. My innocence is worth more than a quid! What's left of it anyway –

TANWANT. We do oil-water blessing when we take journey. Fill blessing tank. When I best village girl, I make lot money as bless tank attendant –

(Car honks again outside.)

(Shouts.) Reita, I getting late!

REITA. *(Shouts, offstage.)* I... can't find the oil... one minute!

TANWANT. I dream this day when I left all lone in Punjab. I no do without you.

PINKY. I wouldn't have done it without you. Tanni, I did it with Tej last night.

TANWANT. Hai Rabba.

PINKY. He loved my bikini wax.

TANWANT. *(Holding up her hand.)* Nahi, no tell me now –

(Unseen by PINKY, REITA walks in carrying a glass of water and open bottle of mustard oil.)

PINKY. Pain was worth it. Brought us even closer together... Til he turned over, left me alone there. *(Checking her phone.)* He must be busy organising your stuff, still hasn't messaged –

REITA. *(Holds up the oil.)* Found it. *(To PINKY..)* Brought who closer together?

PINKY. *(Looking at TANWANT.)* A ...a client. I was... chattin'... to... a client... on the phone... she said... how much her husband loved your bikini waxes –

TANWANT. I getting late –

REITA. *(Putting down the water and oil.)* Which client?

PINKY. Didn't catch her name.

REITA. You had a bikini wax? For a boy?

PINKY. No.

TANWANT. I getting so late.

> (**TANWANT** *tries to open the door.* **REITA** *stops her.)*

REITA. *(To* **TANWANT.***)* You did it?

TANWANT. I got to go.

REITA. *(Blocking* **TANWANT.***)* Did you do it?

> *(The car horn sounds again.)*

TANWANT. Reita, I …

PINKY. I made her do it.

TANWANT. I so sorry. I try tell her I no do. You know no easy say no when Pinky want something –

PINKY. *(To* **REITA.***)* It wasn't her fault.

REITA. *(To* **TANWANT.***)* Why didn't you refuse?

TANWANT. She do me big favour. I repay favour –

PINKY. Oh Tanni –

REITA. A favour?

TANWANT. She give me number for fake husband, fake loan.

REITA. *(To* **PINKY.***)* *You* gave –? Breaking the law too?

PINKY. A friend helped do it.

REITA. Same 'friend' who paid for your tattoos? Did the bikini wax for?

PINKY. Another friend.

TANWANT. *(To* **REITA.***)* What else I do, hain?

REITA. Risking my business –!

TANWANT. You know I always big risk. *(green)*

REITA. – risking her – if you had a 15-year-old daughter, you would have said no.

TANWANT. Pinky family to me –

REITA. She's my daughter. And you – are not a mother.

　　　　(Pause.)

TANWANT. I no mother when I put jahar poison inside me? No mother when my tiny daughter lie dead in my palm?

REITA. A mother doing what's best for you?

PINKY. *(To* **REITA.***)* Like you haven't spent your life doing what's best for you?

TANWANT. Her father who promise everything, force to run. How I struggle lone?

REITA. By killing your daughter?

TANWANT. She be born in better life –

REITA. If that's what you believe.

TANWANT. With baby there, I nothing. As girl there, she nothing. Here, I scrape something. Pinky help. My hand tied. I say no wax, no run after boys, study, no throw way GDPE's like shc do –

PINKY. Tanni –

TANWANT. *(To* **REITA.***)* I say her go back school. Did you?

REITA. 'Back' …?

PINKY. After you made me reschedule my work experience update at school for today – that's what she means.

TANWANT. Pinky, bas. Just tell her.

      (**REITA** *glares at* **PINKY.**)

PINKY. I got kicked out of school.

REITA. Why?

PINKY. Hardly turned up.

REITA. When did –?

PINKY. Few weeks ago.

REITA. But you're on work experience? … Exams coming up…?

      (**PINKY** *is silent. The car honks a few times outside.*)

(*To* **TANWANT.**) Why didn't you tell me?

TANWANT. You her mother. Know your daughter. Know your husband. No just what they show you. No just what you want to see. Reita, I hope you forgive me. I no proud what I do. But for my daughter (*Pause.*) – I has to go.

      (**REITA** *steps aside.* **TANWANT** *leaves.*)

PINKY. It's her wedding day.

REITA. But you still made her give you a bikini wax? (*Pause.*) You're underage.

PINKY. I'm not a kid.

REITA. You can never get it back.

PINKY. Why would I?

REITA. Who was it? Brain-addled crack addict from the train tracks? His pants hung low?

PINKY. Yeah.

REITA. Can't even tell if you're lying or telling the truth.

PINKY. Too late to wonder now.

REITA. Don't you want an education? To train in the Salon? Run your own business?

PINKY. You think I'm gonna take after you? That ain't ever gonna happen! I'm not gonna be stuck in a sad, sham marriage, looking after people's stinky feet, scrubbing off their rough bits, ripping out pubes and smelly underarm hair, pulling hair out of their arses when I'm 60!

REITA. Why make someone else's life less ugly?

PINKY. Think you make people beautiful? You're kidding them, kidding yourself. Living and working a lie. Like Dad says, you're good at that –

REITA. I worked hard to get here – not your Dad. I did all this for you, the boys – so my children never worry about money like I did. I built this Salon. I'm buying a new house for you all –

PINKY. For you!

REITA. You've been given everything. But don't know the value of anything, not even yourself. Giving your body so cheaply to the first boy who flatters you?

PINKY. A man.

REITA. Oh God.

PINKY. I wanted to.

REITA. You're a kid! Not old enough to know what you want –

PINKY. I'll be happier than you, richer than you –

REITA. I've got my own business, an education –

PINKY. You couldn't even get into college –

REITA. For a girl from India, who never spoke English, I studied hard, worked hard –

PINKY. Oh for fuck's sake –

REITA. – I studied hard, worked hard –

PINKY. BD gave you the money to open this Salon –

REITA. I used my Mum's money too. I've supported your Dad, raised his three kids –

PINKY. You didn't do that alone. BD raised us too.

REITA. I didn't bring you up to turn out like this –

PINKY. Don't worry, I can count houses, lip-line –

REITA. You've never had to struggle or fight a day in your life for anything. I lost my Mum at your age, had to learn English in a foreign country, fit into a white school, white town –

PINKY. You know what? I don't want to know – cos I don't care! So they tugged your plaits and called you 'Paki'! Boo hoo! Said you had greasy hair! Boo hoo! You know what? You did –

> (**PINKY** *grabs the oil and pours it over* **REITA***'s head, greasing it down over her scalp.*)

– cos your Mum came from a fucking backwards little village in smelly India and didn't know when to stop pouring oil over your head! Yeah, they spat at you, cos you're a stupid Paki Freshie who deserved it. It's been decades – get over it. If it fucked up your sad little life, it makes no fucking difference to mine!

> (**PINKY** *hurls the bottle at the mirror, cracking it.* **REITA** *wipes away dripping oil.*)

REITA. You never met my Mum. I'm glad. I'd have been ashamed to call you my daughter in front of her.

PINKY. Like I fucking care.

> (**PINKY** *storms out of the Salon, slamming the door. Bits of ceiling rain down. Dripping in*

oil, **REITA** *looks on after her. Lights dim. In a sunset glow,* **REITA** *takes the photograph from the drawer and sticks it on the cracked mirror. She picks up her mother's surma bottle, cleans the surma stick and dips it into the bottle. In her broken reflection, she streaks her eyes, pink to black, tracing the cracks in the glass. She takes out her phone, typing a message. Light knocking on the door.* **REITA** *hangs up and opens the door to* **BIG DHADHI.***)*

BIG DHADHI. Why you got tel in your hair, all over your kaprey?

REITA. Pinky head massage.

  *(***BIG DHADHI*** sits down. Pause.)*

Sangeeta?

BIG DHADHI. No open box. No see her face.

REITA. *(Bowing her head.)* Body too cut up?

BIG DHADHI. Husband there. His family there.

REITA. Other man too?

BIG DHADHI. Eh ni mainu pata. But poor husband, he broken –

REITA. They said that about my Dad too.

BIG DHADHI. We not know what happen.

REITA. I do.

  (Pause.)

I'm 15, Mum won't let me talk to the Ahmed boy on our street. In case Dad sees. Tells me off in front of the boy. So I tell Dad I saw Mum flirt with a neighbour.

BIG DHADHI. Your Mummyji never paagal woman people say.

REITA. Lock myself in my room. Slide on my headphones. Turn the music up so loud, so I can't hear him shout at her.

BIG DHADHI. I marry you to Harmeet, so you be daughter I never has.

(Crying, **REITA** *takes* **BIG DHADHI***'s hand.)*

REITA. I dance in my room. From my window, I see her walk down the garden path, past her marigolds, roses, lotus seeds, fresh in the soil. White chunni fluttering in the wind. She dries her tears with it. Walks through the gate. Turns. Looks up to my window. I see her. She doesn't see me. She never comes back. Because of me.

BIG DHADHI. *(Wiping* **REITA***'s tears.)* You no blame.

REITA. I believed everything Dad told me.

BIG DHADHI. You be young, like Pinky.

REITA. She was too young – for wrinkles, white hairs he ripped out, clump by clump. He would drag her about. Pull her this way. Hurl her that way. Her body limp. Her hair, broken white threads. I'd drop to the floor with her, curl into a ball, so she'd see me – and he wouldn't. Whirl the broken hair, into a tangled web around her. He'd shout at me. Point a finger at her... Til I did the same.

BIG DHADHI. Nahi, you no blame.

*(***BIG DHADHI*** holds* **REITA***. Pause.)*

Your Mummyji pop lotus seed in Punjab, like me. She try grow them in park, near pond... Tell me story once. 'Bhanji, lotus root grow in mud but mud no touch lotus flower. Frog sit on lotus leaf, think he so clever – he swim in mud, jump, drink, eat, roll round in mud. But frog never know lotus flower so close, to feed him, make him more happy – he never know lotus beauty all round him.'

REITA. She'd tell me that story too.

BIG DHADHI. She always say me you her lotus beauty.

REITA. Truth is, I've always been the frog.

BIG DHADHI. *(Chuckling.)* We all is. *(Pause.)* Before your Mummyji, after, womans still jump. Our kuriyah, mundey, come from there, jump here. We see train stop, police, ambulance...but too quick, we shut box, so tight, no talk. Our kuriyah, mundey jump cos they no fit here. Has no more fight to fit here...

REITA. I always wanted to fit in –

BIG DHADHI. *(Stroking her beard.)* I proud I no fit in.

> *(**REITA** smiles, squeezes **BIG DHADHI**'s hand.)*

Take house.

REITA. What?

BIG DHADHI. All your and Harmeet anyway.

REITA. BD – *(Pause.)* I put in an offer yesterday. I'm meant to see the Councillor *(Checks the time on her phone.)* soon, put down a deposit, sign on the dotted line...

BIG DHADHI. Sign.

> *(The door rattles. Bits of ceiling fall to the floor.)*

(Smiling.) Shavaash! *(Touching her heart.)* There he is. Say sign too.

> *(**TANWANT** pushes open the door. Clutching the keys, she stops in the doorway.)*

TANWANT. Ho. I no think anyone be –

BIG DHADHI. Vadhaiyan khurio!

TANWANT. *(Welling up.)* I come in? Change clothe?

(*REITA nods. TANWANT walks in, tearfully.*)

BIG DHADHI. (*Holding out her arms.*) Jhapi deh. You
married womans now.

> (*TANWANT shakes her head and tries not to
> cry in BIG DHADHI's arms.*)

Haah Tanni, aa ki hoya?

> (*TANWANT gathers herself and holds out the
> Salon keys for REITA.*)

TANWANT. I pick up all my thing from shed, give you shed
key after.

REITA. (*Taking the keys.*) What happened?

TANWANT. (*Holding back tears.*) I no risk. No risk.

REITA. Tanni –

> (*Pause. TANWANT composes herself.*)

TANWANT. No husband. No agent. No-one. Just me.
All lone, on step, in too tight second-hand lengha.
Everyone stare me. No-one see me.

BIG DHADHI. (*Comforting TANWANT.*) Ho puth.

> (*PINKY rushes into the Salon.*)

PINKY. (*To TANWANT.*) I've been calling you – why didn't
you –?

> (*TANWANT is too upset to speak.*)

Was he there? Like he said?

> (*TANWANT bows her head.*)

I called him. So many times. No answer. He didn't pick
up...didn't pick up...didn't...then his number just...
stopped...working...

REITA. Pinky.

TANWANT. *(To* **REITA.***)* I get clothe. Then, go home, pack.

PINKY. *(To* **TANWANT.***)* I'm so sorry.

> *(***TANWANT** *heads into the cubicle. Silence.)*

Don't let her go Mum. Please don't let her go. She doesn't have anywhere to go.

REITA. Help Tanni out of her lengha

PINKY. I'm so sorry.

> *(***PINKY** *heads into the cubicle.)*

BIG DHADHI. You no let Tanni go.

> *(***REITA** *exhales, holding her head.)*

And Pinky – she need shittar. More like her Daddyji than she know.

REITA. Or more like her Mummyji?

BIG DHADHI. My son no sadhu saint. He do nothing 'cept live his best life. Like frog.

> *(***REITA** *smiles. She checks her phone, then puts it away. She picks up the overturned bottle of oil from the floor, walks to the drawer and takes out a key, holding it out for* **BIG DHADHI.***)*

REITA. Your house key.

BIG DHADHI. I keep?

> *(***REITA** *nods.* **BIG DHADHI** *blesses* **REITA***, touching her head. Dressed in casual clothes,* **TANWANT** *comes back out, followed by a tearful* **PINKY.** *Pause.)*

(To **REITA.***)* You no late for house meeting?

> *(***REITA** *looks at her phone and nods.)*

No go?

REITA. I don't know BD.

BIG DHADHI. Trust Waheguru – answer will come.

PINKY. *(Wiping her tears.)* But Mum, you really wanted –

REITA. *(To* **PINKY.***)* Walk Tanni home. Pamper her. Preen her. Don't let her leave.

TANWANT. Thank you Reita.

> (**TANWANT** *and* **PINKY** *begin heading out.* **TANWANT** *leaves.* **PINKY** *turns back.)*

PINKY. Mum – I saw Kamal on the way here, with her daughter. Rushing to the station. I called out. She ignored me. She didn't look good.

BIG DHADHI. Haan, I see Kamal Saas after funeral. But no do chugali gossip *(Covering her mouth with her chunni.)* –

REITA. BD ...?

BIG DHADHI. Her Saas, her husband very angry. No find Kamal, Gaggan anywhere.

REITA. You didn't tell them you saw Kamal earlier?

BIG DHADHI. Nahi.

REITA. She'll be back home by now –

PINKY. She looked really upset Mum.

> (**PINKY** *leaves.)*

BIG DHADHI. *(To* **REITA.***)* Go station. Check hain? Poor girl need someone. Challo –

REITA. I can't –

BIG DHADHI. Let nother woman suffer?

REITA. I haven't been there – since –

BIG DHADHI. What if someone do for your Mummyji?

Closing

(A red sunset glow washes over the train platform. Fast trains shoot past. **KAMAL** *stands on the platform, with Gaggan in a pram, the pram perilously close to the yellow edge.* **KAMAL** *closes her eyes, holds out her hand and breathes as a train rushes by. Pause. Another train approaches in the far distance.)*

KAMAL. Gaggan, can you see the train coming? Look closely. See the lights? Amber lights. You ready to go? Strapped in? Ready to be a brave girl for Mummyji?

*(***KAMAL*** pushes the pram forward.* **REITA** *appears on another platform.)*

REITA. *(Shouts.)* Please, somebody stop her! Kamal, stand back! Pull back the pram! Get away from the edge! ... Mummyji, get away from the edge!

(Freeze. **REITA** *closes her eyes. Long pause. A train shoots past, fading into silence. A cold rush washes over* **REITA**. *Pause. She opens her eyes, bows her head and sees a pink lotus at her feet. She picks it up, holds it, breathes it in.)*

She's gone... She's gone...

(Lights out.)

GLOSSARY

HUNNAH? – right?/Isn't it?

DESI – native to India/Punjab/one's home 'desh' country; homegrown

NAHI – no

HAI – expression of pain or alarm

BHAJI – brother

HAIN – what? or adds emphasis to a question

THAVA – flat iron griddle pan for making chappatis

ROTI – chappati (flat round bread) cooked on a thava (griddle pan)

CHOTTE – fat/plump

GORI/GORA – white

RANG – colour

KULCHA – traditional Punjabi soft, round flatbread, usually stuffed with vegetables, paneer or meat and spices

GUPSHUP – chit chat/gossip

EHNI THAND – so cold

APNAY – our

EK DHUM – immediately/at once

RABBA – God

SAT SRI AKAL – Sikh greeting in Punjabi, roughly translated as 'True is the timeless one'.

SACHI? – really?

HANJI/HAAN – yes

MEHNDI – henna hand and body decoration

TIKKA – traditional piece of head jewellery worn in the hair parting, on the forehead

NATH – traditional piece of nose jewellery – a nose stud or nose ring, with a long gold chain attached to the ear

LENGHA – traditional ankle-length (wedding) skirt/outfit

LUCHI-KUTHI-KAMINI-HARAMJADI-RANDI – vagrant-bitch-scoundrel-bastard-prostitute

HO – oh

WAHEGURU – God; the Supreme Being

FRESHIE – pejorative slang for an illegal immigrant 'fresh off the boat'

ATTA – chapatti flour/dough

THEEK YA – that's fine/right/alright

PAAGAL – mad/crazy

SHAADI – wedding/marriage

JALDI – quickly/hurry

GAL SUN – listen to me/hear me out

CHAPPALS – pair of Indian slippers or sandals

ANGREZ – English

DIL – heart

SHALWAR KAMEEZ – traditional women's dress consisting of a pair of loose, light, ankle-cuffed shalwar trousers and a long kameez tunic top

EHNA SOHNA – so handsome

THUSI MAINU BELIEVE NAHI KARENGE – you won't believe me

CHAKKI – millstones to grind corn/wheat into flour

DUPATTA – a long scarf or shawl worn by women over the head and shoulders, usually with a matching shalwar kameez outfit

GIDDHA – women's traditional folk/harvest dance in Punjab, energetically performed in circles, to rhythmic clapping and boliyan (traditional folk songs)

CHAA – Indian tea with milk, sugar and spices

BARFI – variously coloured, dense milk-based Indian sweets, flavoured with fruit, nuts, spices

CHHOTE – tiny/little

MERI KISMET – my fate/my destiny

HAAAH – expression of fear/alarm

DHAKKAY MAARDI SARAA DHIN – pushes (me) around all day

DHAKKA – push

AAJA – come on

THORA RAAM KAR – take a little rest

EHNAY GUNDAY – such dirty

DHARI – beard

MAIN TUHANU DASSDI – I tell you

SHITTARRI DI KACHI – you should be skinned alive or slapped/beaten raw

THAP – beat/throb

MERE GODHAY – my knees

LEHJAA – take it

KI? – what?

BAS – enough/stop

PUTHE KAM – bad things

DI LAGDI – mocking a girl/woman for saying/doing/being something

EHNA/EHNI – so/such a

EH NI MAINU PATA – I don't know about that

PAKKA – settled

SHARAM KAR – have some shame

CHAUKAREE – posture of sitting cross-legged

KHOON – blood

BAHUTH VADI BECHARI – (sarcastically) Oh such a poor woman!

DUKH-SUKH – ups and downs/Pain-pleasure

GAL SUNDI AA – Do you hear me?

HARAMJADA – bastard

SABJI – vegetables

ACHAA – various meanings, depending on usage – oh really/ok/right/good/I see/understand/so

VADHAIYAN – congratulations

PASHOO IN THE PIND – cattle in the village

EK – one

MUNDEY – boys

KHURIO/KHURIYA – girl/girls

CHUPRI (ROTI) – buttered (roti)

CHHIL – peel/skin

THORI SHARAM KAR – have a little shame

SAADI – our

KHEER – Indian rice pudding made with rice, milk, sugar, cardamom and nuts

BECHARA/BECHARI – poor man/woman

SAHI GAL – true say/true words/agreed

PUTHAR/PUTH – affectionate term for a beloved son (sometimes also daughter)

AJJ – today

KHATAM – finished/done

NAPP – press

CHADD/CHADDO – leave it

KARVA CHAUTH – one day festival to celebrate the bond of marriage, in which married Hindu women fast for the long life, health and prosperity of their husbands

OM – a sacred syllable and spiritual symbol in the Hindu religion (also, in Tibetan Buddhism and Jainism)

EK ONKAR – a sacred symbol, central tenet of Sikhism and the opening words of the Sikh holy book the Guru Granth Sahib, meaning 'There is One God'

SEVA – selfless (religious/spiritual) service; a central tenet of Sikhism

GURUJIS – the 10 Sikh Gurus

SAAS – mother-in-law

REHNDE – leave it

PARAY HO – move aside

LANGAR – Sikh communal free kitchen, which serves free, vegetarian meals to all, regardless of faith

BHAR – weight

AMB – mango

MERE HATH JORHE – my hands are folded

CHUNNI – a long scarf worn by women over the head and shoulders, usually with a matching shalwar kameez outfit

BAS KAR – stop it/enough is enough

SHARAM – shame

ITHAY AA – come here

PATILA – cooking pot

LATHI – a long, heavy stick used as a weapon

AMRIT – sacred sweetened Sikh water used in the Amrit baptism ceremony and for other religious purposes, means 'nectar'

BAKWAAS NA KAR – don't talk rubbish/nonsense

KITHO? – where from?

PHUDIS – slang for vaginas

DUR FITTEH MOOH – an expression of annoyance, ridicule, exasperation, akin to a face-palm, when someone does something stupid or something goes wrong; roughly, get your slapped face away from here

PAJ – run

KOTHI – big Punjabi house or mansion

KHICH – pull

PAAL – raise/bring up

EHNI DHAR – so scared

CHITTA – white

JADI THAND – too cold

BAZAAR – an Indian market

MALA – prayer beads

KAPREY – clothes

KAPREY LAH – take off your clothes

CHAKKAR – dizziness

KACCHERA – cotton shorts/underpants, one of the Sikh 5 Ks (religious symbols), symbolising purity and chastity (and once offering Sikh soldiers mobility in warfare)

KIRPAN – small ceremonial dagger, one of the Sikh 5 Ks, symbolising the fight against injustice and oppression

NANGI – naked

SHINK – sprinkle/dab

DAVAI – medicine

RANI – Queen

KALIRE – half-coconut or umbrella shaped dangling wedding accessory, usually made from gold metallic foil and tied to the choora, symbolising sustenance, wealth, prosperity in the new marital home

CHOORA – a set of red and white wedding bangles, gifted by a maternal uncle and aunt, traditionally purified in milk, symbolising marriage, luck, fertility and prosperity

VADIYA – good/alright

VOTI – bride

DEKHO – look

KIDDA? – informal greeting meaning 'How are you?'

THUSI – you (polite form)

CHALDI – goes on/continues

NANIJI – granny (maternal side – mother's mother)

CHUP KAR – shut up/be quiet

PYAAR – love/blessing

BAHUTH – such/a lot of

MOOH BHAND – mouth shut

HAAR – necklace

JAHAR – poison

TEL – oil

BHANJI – colloquial term for 'sister'

SHAVAASH – well done, bravo

JHAPI DEH – give me a hug

AA KI HOYA? – What's happened here?

SHITTAR – slaps/beats

CHUGALI – gossip

CHALLO – go

Lightning Source UK Ltd.
Milton Keynes UK
UKHW020700080522
402641UK00003B/7